I'D RATHER DIE THAN GIVE A SPEECH

This book is humbly and gratefully dedicated to my business partner and lifelong friend, Mary Tavon, who is easily the hardest working individual on this planet, and who not only ran our firm while I finished this work but also helped edit it.

I'D RATHER DIE THAN GIVE A SPEECH

Michael M. Klepper
with Robert E. Gunther

A Citadel Press Book
Published by Carol Publishing Group

Carol Publishing Group Edition, 1995

A Citadel Press Book
Published by Carol Publishing Group
Citadel Press is a registered trademark of Carol Communications, Inc.

Editorial Offices: 600 Madison Avenue, New York, NY 10022
Sales & Distribution Offices: 120 Enterprise Avenue, Secaucus, NJ 07094
In Canada: Canadian Manda Group, One Atlantic Avenue, Suite 105
Toronto, Ontario, M6K 3E7

Queries regarding rights and permissions should be addressed to:
Carol Publishing Group, 600 Madison Avenue, New York, NY 10022

Manufactured in the United States of America
10 9 8 7 6 5 4 3 2 1

Carol Publishing Group books are available at special discounts for bulk purchases, sales promotions, fund raising, or educational purposes. Special editions can also be created to specifications. For details contact: Special Sales Department, Carol Publishing Group, 120 Enterprise Ave., Secaucus, NJ 07094

Library of Congress Cataloging-in-Publication Data

Klepper, Michael M.
     I'd rather die than give a speech! : turn anxious moments into rewarding experiences / by Michael M. Klepper with Robert Gunther ; foreword by Edwin Newman.
     p. cm.
     "A Citadel Press book."
     ISBN 0-8065-1616-X
     1. Public speaking—Handbooks, manuals, etc. I. Gunther, Robert E., 1960– . II. Title.
PN4121.K662   1995
808.5'1—dc20   94-44941
                                                              CIP

Foreword

It's strange.

The United States unquestionably has more public speaking than any other country in the world. Politicians do it, of course, and teachers, and clerics, and people in the business world, and lecturers. That last group is especially important. The size of the American lecture market is vast and not even remotely approached anywhere else. It goes back, with us, to the latter part of the 19th century. As the frontier moved farther west, a "lecture circuit" took shape, with speakers going out from cities in the east to keep settlers abreast of things, speaking to them about any number of subjects. For many, attending these lectures was a form of adult education, and the lecturing tradition helped to solidify the place of public speaking in the country.

And yet—and this is what is strange—in this unrivaled arena of public speaking, the level of that speaking is low, depressingly and unnecessarily low. Why? A number of reasons. In politics, it is largely because, outside the legislative halls, politicians almost always speak to captive audiences, and while inside those halls, politicians do not have the cut and thrust, the extemporaneous duels common in parliamentary countries. We have, for example, nothing like the British Prime Minister's question time, with the House of Commons full of cheers and jeers and the Speaker shouting, often vainly, "Order, order!" Indeed, thanks to C-Span, we even see members of Congress speak to empty chambers so as to get their remarks into the *Congressional Record*.

Outside of politics, the reason public speaking so often fails is because of elementary mistakes, the most fundamental of which is regarding a speech as something to be survived or a painful chore. There seems to be no understanding of the importance of presentation, of varying the delivery, of pausing now and then for emphasis, of putting oneself in the audience's place, and above all, of preparing properly. I have even seen speakers who ignore the location of the microphone and speak three or four feet away from it. In short, too many of those who speak are boring, and their speeches are often useless.

These are matters to which Michael Klepper addresses himself: Preparing and writing a speech, delivering it, and realizing that it does not have to be an ordeal. It is an opportunity, and if the opportunity is grasped and the response is the one hoped for, it can be immensely satisfying—even a pleasure.

Edwin Newman

Acknowledgments

This book would never have been undertaken were it not for the support and contributions of some extraordinary people:

- CEO Robert J. Baer of United Van Lines, who believed in my techniques, used them, and insisted his managers do the same; and his Director of Corporate Communications, Cliff Saxton, who made sure they did.
- American Management Association Chairman Dr. Tom Horton, who once introduced me as "the best speech trainer in the business."
- A high-level executive at one of the Big Three automakers, who reacted to my techniques by saying, "I had the words, you gave me the music."
- An attorney, who, after attending one of my programs and implementing some of the ideas, reported that he was now so confident that I'd actually changed his life.
- Those many senior communications and public relations executives such as Brad Carr at the New York State Bar Association, Donna Vandiver at Monsanto, and Howard Charbeneau at E G & G Mound, who, year after year, have entrusted me with their top management.
- Boys Town Executive Director Father Val Peter, Vice President Tom Gregory, Director of Development Tom Schuyler, and Public Relations Director Randy Blauvelt, who have all gone through our training programs and insist that other Boys Town executives do the same.
- Greyhound Lines, Inc., President and CEO Frank Schmieder and Public Relations Director Liz Dunn for their ongoing support and bus bank mementos!

- Jack Smith, himself an author, former features editor of the "Today Show," and, as of this writing, a lecturer in writing journalism at Gilbert College in Greensboro, North Carolina. Throughout my life, he has been a major source of encouragement and inspiration.
- And finally, to my editor Cynthia Zigmund, without whose patience, fortitude and vision, this book would still be languishing in my word processor.

Preface

If your palms are sweating on these pages, you're going to have to purchase this book. Not because you're making the ink run (although that may be reason enough), but because this volume contains proven techniques that can calm your nerves and help you make a speech or presentation that sings. It can help you survive—and I hope even enjoy—the experience.

(If you don't believe me, I'm living proof that petrifying terror can be transformed into knock-out speechmaking. The story of my transformation is in the introduction.)

Whether you're the CEO talking to the entire corporation or a manager making a pitch to senior executives, whether you are speaking to a convention hall full of auto dealers or a conference room full of doctors, the simple techniques presented here will give you an edge in getting your message out.

This book represents the accumulated wisdom of decades of teeth-chattering stage fright followed by decades of delivering speeches and training hundreds of executives to deliver them. These techniques have been tried and tested in the crucible of many spotlights, microphones, and meeting rooms.

You will learn how to craft a speech that can seize the audience's attention from the first syllable and hold it through your last word. You will learn how to stand and deliver—everything from eye contact to energy level. You will learn how to handle the question-and-answer period (Q&A) at the end of the speech to reinforce your key points. Along the way, we'll examine grabbers, road maps, the importance of ear appeal, and how to use humor, numbers, and visuals. You'll learn why you should arrive early, what questions to expect, and how to avoid getting into debates with hostile questioners.

You can read through this book long before you have to give a speech. Or you can work through each section with your speech draft in hand. Some of you may try to use all the techniques here at once, but even if you gradually add one or two with each speech, you'll notice an improvement.

I don't know anyone who has actually died from giving a speech. There are more hazardous ways to spend an afternoon. Most of us end up better for having survived, and when you hear the audience's applause, you will probably feel stronger and more confident. But you only get one shot—only one chance to make that first impression.

So now, you're on.

Michael Klepper

The Big Decision

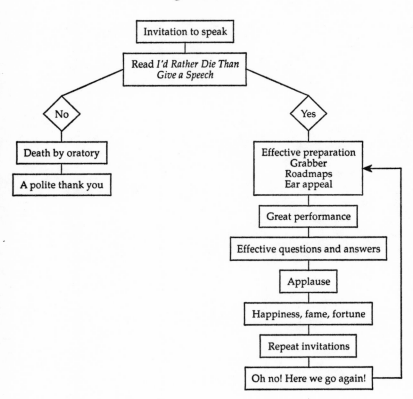

Contents

Introduction
From Heart Failure to Speeches with Heart

My boss called me into his office.

"We're pitching the Clairol account. It could be an important major piece of new business for us, our first consumer client. I want you on the presenting team to discuss the broadcast media."

What could I say? No one knew the agony I went through when someone asked me to present. *"I'd rather die than give a speech,"* I thought to myself.

It started when I was a child. My mother would take me to birthday parties. But before they would give out the cake and goodies, each child was required to sing, dance, play an instrument, tell a story, or "recite." I was petrified, afraid I'd make a fool of myself. I did. I'd run to the bathroom, lock the door, and hide. It got so bad that I eventually told my mother: "No more parties!"

That fear of presenting carried over into my adult life. Whenever I was told I'd have to present my ideas to an audience, fear overcame me.

Before I was introduced, I'd begin to sweat profusely. My heart would pound. I was convinced anyone sitting next to me could hear it and would think they were in the neighborhood of a runaway bass drum.

I've since learned I'm not alone. Many executives called on to make presentations before such groups as boards of directors, analysts, stockholders, regulators, employees, or franchisees

1

experience some form of apprehension, some form of concern. We've all heard stories about even veteran show business personalities going through various stages of nervousness—from sweating to palpitations to vomiting—before going on.

Except for the vomiting, all the rest aptly described me.

In addition, I couldn't believe the sound of my own voice. My throat became dry and so constricted that my words sounded like they were being sung by a soprano.

A TURNING POINT

But with this latest "command performance" decreed by my boss, I vowed to somehow overcome my agony. I spent the entire weekend writing my ideas. Then I distilled the ones I planned to showcase into a well-organized, easy-to-follow presentation.

Then I rehearsed. Oh, did I rehearse. I locked myself in my room and recited my thoughts aloud over and over again, firmly implanting them in my mind's ear. As I listened to them, I could tell which ideas made sense and which wouldn't work. I highlighted the former and deleted the latter.

On the day I was to present my thoughts, I noticed I was still nervous, but not nearly as nervous as I had been in the past. I rehearsed a few more times in my office during the morning. The now familiar words came easily.

At the meeting, I was still somewhat apprehensive, but I found myself looking forward to my five minutes. When my turn came, the words flowed. I was easily able to make eye contact with the prospects. My energy level was high. I was enthusiastic. At the very least, I could sense that the Clairol people knew that I believed in my ideas. From the intensity of their return gazes, I could tell they were closely following every word I said.

When the presentation was over, people came up to tell me how intrigued they were with my recommendations.

One of my fellow presenters came up and said, "That was one heck of a show, my man."

And it was. I knew it was. The prospective client knew it was. My fellow workers knew it was.

I wish I could say we got the account. Sadly, we didn't. But I had personally managed to hurdle what could have been a career handicap and turned it into a career asset.

Looking back at that important moment in my life, I realize I had instinctively done what I now teach:

- I spoke about a topic I not only knew but knew well and was passionate about.
- From first word to last, there was an easy-to-follow, logical flow to my material.
- I was prepared. I was rehearsed. I was confident. I was enthusiastic.

Now, I'd like to share with you the techniques I learned then—and many others I've learned since.

A ROAD MAP FOR THIS BOOK

A little later, we'll examine the importance of road maps in speeches. But you'll need a map to get there. This book, like many effective speeches, is designed around a triad: preparation, performance, and post-presentation.

In the first part, we'll examine the key ingredients in preparing an effective speech—including structure, texture, and technique. Structure deals with seizing the audience's attention with a "grabber," using road maps, and then tying it all up. Texture deals with the feel of the speech, such as "ear appeal," imagery, putting yourself into the speech, and using humor and numbers. Technique deals with the hows of creating a speech, from understanding your audience, to using visuals, to working with speechwriters. We'll deal with details from how long your first draft should be to when to use cards or text. In all, the first part of the book covers everything you need to consider before you walk into the room.

In Part II, we'll look at the delivery of the speech, the actual performance, from arriving early to making last-minute adjustments. Finally, in Part III, we will look at how to successfully handle the post-presentation Q&A.

Remember, the three key steps are preparation, presentation, and post–presentation.

At the end of each chapter is a Chapter Checklist that highlights the key ideas to keep in mind. Similarly, there is a Death by Oratory section with cautions about things to avoid if you value your life (or at least your pride).

PREPARATION

"A good impromptu speech takes about three weeks to prepare."

Mark Twain

P reparation is the key to an effective speech. Once you are up in front of that audience, you have only one shot at success. But before you begin, there is no limit to how much time you can spend preparing.

There is a story about a research assistant who prepared a background briefing for Henry Kissinger. The assistant spent a week slaving over the numbers and reports, putting together his best work for the venerable Dr. Kissinger. He sent the report in, and in less than an hour it came back with a quickly written message that the author could do better. The assistant redoubled his efforts and after a week of working late nights, he again turned in the report. But it came back quickly again with a note that it still needed more work. After spending another week sweating over the report, the assistant asked to deliver it personally to Dr. Kissinger. He told Kissinger that it was the best possible report he could produce, and he had spent three weeks of sleepless nights honing it.

"Very good," Kissinger replied. "Now I'll read it."

Even if you don't have Henry Kissinger to drive you, this kind of relentless preparation is very important to a successful speech. You may not always have a lot of time to give to the preparation of a speech. Nonetheless, giving the speech some thought several weeks or months before the event can help you come up with effective approaches to the subject. You will probably spend some time thinking about the speech, if only to worry about it. Why not use this time more productively?

In this chapter, we examine effective ways to use the time before you step up to the podium. We will offer pointers on shaping and developing your speech so that your audience will have no choice but to listen. Specifically, we will look at three areas:

- Structure—approaches to designing your speech.
- Texture—the texture of the words and stories you stretch over this frame.
- Technique—the thousands of details that go into researching and creating the speech.

STRUCTURE

An effective presentation is one that makes it easy for people to follow the speaker's thinking from first word to last. It's organized. It's orderly.

Speeches have a beginning, middle, and end. That may sound self-evident, but you'd be surprised how many people forget this. They start the speech without starting it, they meander in the middle, or they trail off without a strong conclusion.

The beginning should seize the attention of the audience with a grabber. The middle should keep them on track with a road map. The end should draw it all together.

A speech without structure is like a human body without a

skeleton. It won't stand. Spineless. Like a jellyfish. You get the picture. Having structure won't make the speech a great one, but lacking structure will surely kill all the inspired thoughts that are contained in the speech because listeners are too busy trying to find out where they are to pay attention to the speech.

Chapter One

Speech Strategy
Why Give a Speech?

T his book is primarily designed to tell you how to give a speech. But before you consider *how* to give a speech, you must first determine *why*. If you are giving a speech to fill time, that is all you will do.

Speeches, after all, are only air. But what you do with this air is up to you. You can leave your audience sweltering and frazzled by a 20-minute monsoon—or you can take them on a balloon ride. The raw materials are the same; the results are quite different. One thing is certain. They won't come along unless you know where you want to take them.

DO YOU WANT TO CHANGE THE WORLD?

The Gettysburg address changed the world without any bells and whistles. It was like a stealth attack. It slipped into people's minds and hearts, transforming a nation.

Lincoln simply had the right words at the right time. Our founding fathers never really intended the phrase "all men are created equal" to refer to anything more than "all white males." Lincoln changed all that with just 272 words.

Not every speech is intended to transform nations or move an audience to tears. What do you want the audience to do at the close of the speech? Do you want them to go out and cast a vote, buy your product, feel good about you, about your company, about themselves? Do you want to create a sense of frustration or instill a sense of hope?

There are as many purposes to an oral presentation as there are speakers. Some speeches are meant primarily to entertain, others to inform, others to defend. Some are rallying cries, designed to incite a riot or launch a thousand ships. Some are designed to draw a smile or get people thinking, others are calls for action.

If you don't know where you are headed with your speech, you will probably wind up somewhere else. There is a story about Albert Einstein that illustrates this point. Einstein was riding a train to New York when the conductor asked him for his ticket. The absent-minded Einstein began going through his briefcase. The conductor, recognizing him, quickly said, "No problem, Dr. Einstein" and walked on. When he came back, Einstein had the contents of two briefcases unloaded on the seat. The conductor once again assured him that the ticket was "no big deal." The scientist responded, "Maybe for you it's not important, but if I don't find that ticket, how will I know where to get off?"

You're the train engineer. You will deliver the speech. But where you get off is up to you. Where you take this train filled with innocent passengers is up to you.

GO FOR THE HEART

Speeches are sound waves that go out from the speaker across the room and into the ears of the listeners. That part of the speech is a physical process, fairly mundane. No matter what the content of the speech or the delivery, this process of moving air occurs.

But the object is to move more than air. It is to move your listeners. The next stage is to engage the ear. If the ear likes what it is hearing, it will ask for more. It will drink in the sweet melody of the words. Then the brain will wake up and take notice. The brain will start unraveling the messages contained in these sweet words. It will gather the information, follow the road maps, marvel at the language.

Then suddenly, the unsuspecting heart, listening at the door, will overhear something that makes it jump. Now, it is not a speech anymore. It is an experience. This is the magic of speechmaking. The audience is absorbed, spellbound, held in the grasp of your words.

You can't expect this from every speech. You can't expect this from every audience. Sometimes, it is inappropriate. But it is where the speech can penetrate the deepest and have the most impact.

In his 1963 speech at the Lincoln Memorial, Martin Luther King, Jr. created the defining vision of the civil rights movement. When he said "I have a dream," the words resonated in hearts across America.

In his speech proclaiming that "we choose to go to the moon in this decade," John F. Kennedy propelled a nation toward a seemingly impossible goal. It was a vision as powerful as the rockets that eventually delivered Man to the moon.

Or, when standing in a Berlin square in 1963, he said, "Today, in the world of freedom, the proudest boast is 'Ich Bin Ein Berliner.' " That declaration, according to one historian, "touched and heartened the people of West Germany as no other statement could have done. From that moment he had a place in the affections of the free Germans that inspired striking manifestations of grief following his assassination."[1]

The more you put yourself into your speech, the closer your heart is to the speech, the more your audience will be affected by it. The more distance you keep from your ideas, the less impact the speech will have.

Audiences can sense sincerity like dogs sense fear. They know when you are lying. They know when you are speaking about issues you care about. The written word can hide much more. It can be crafted over days, weeks, or years. It can be sweated over. But the spoken word is in real time. Even when the speech is carefully rehearsed, the performance has a directness and authenticity that cannot be matched by print.

Some speeches go for the jugular, others go for the brain. But the most effective ones aim for the heart.

THE ULTERIOR MOTIVE

There are many good reasons why you might want to deliver a speech. There is only one bad reason: Because you were asked and you didn't give it a second thought. Think carefully when you accept an invitation, and even more carefully when you solicit a speaking opportunity, about what it is you want to gain from it. Even Martin Luther King had a clear, personal objective for his speech, regardless of how lofty that objective was.

You need to ask yourself: What's in it for me or for my organization? Among the reasons that might cause you to take to the road and speak are to:

- Promote a cause.
- Improve your image.
- Improve the image of your organization.
- Sell products or services.
- Meet new customers.
- Answer questions.
- Announce a discovery.
- Participate in an important ceremony.
- Revitalize the troops.
- Explain what you're doing and why.

You can do two or three of these things at once. Executives who make speeches on the need for better education can enhance their personal images as well as the images of their companies. At the same time, the speakers promote a cause they strongly believe in. And, finally, they may attract customers who will take another look at their companies because of this enhanced image.

There are many other reasons why people give speeches. The important thing is that you know *your* reason. You can have great technique and not accomplish your goal. You will only accomplish your goal if you know what it is and keep it clearly in front of you.

A TOUCHSTONE

Once you have determined what you want your speech to do, you need to ask yourself at every stage of preparation if the speech will actually achieve your ends. Write your goal down at the top of your speech, on the cover of your speech file. Keep it in front of your mind. Ask yourself: Does the speech end with a clear appeal? Does it make a convincing argument? In this way, you can ensure that what goes into the speech is clearly focused on the task at hand, and that you don't end up crafting a great speech that doesn't get the job done.

Chapter Checklist

Speech Strategy

- What are you attempting to accomplish in the speech? What do you want your audience to do or feel?
- Are you trying to persuade, inform, or entertain?
- Does your speech achieve these ends?
- Before you accept a speaking engagement and all the work it entails, ask yourself, will it work to your advantage?

Death by Oratory

A speech can be well conceived and delivered but lead to the wrong results. Socrates may have delivered one of the world's most memorable speeches to a jury in Athens in 399 B.C. It was brilliantly argued, but it still didn't manage to keep away that cup of hemlock. While everyone was impressed with his defense of truth, the jury still found him guilty of corrupting the young. It has been suggested that the jury resented his unbending pride. Whatever the reason, the speech lasted more than 2,000 years, but Socrates didn't. If he had examined his goals more carefully, he might have found a way to make his point without having to lose his life in the process.

- Don't give a speech until you know what you want to accomplish with your speech. Then test each statement against that touchstone. A speech without a clear purpose will accomplish nothing.

- Don't forget that it is not how your speech affects you that is important—it's how it affects your audience.

- No speech should ever come into the world without a clear purpose. The world is overpopulated with aimlessly wandering discourse as it is.

Chapter Two

Seize Their Attention

The first words out of your mouth set the tone for the entire speech. These words can tune your audience out—"Thank you, Madame Chairperson. It's truly a pleasure being here")—or they can be grabbers.

Grabbing an audience is like catching snakes—if you grab them by the back of the neck, you have them free and clear. But if you miss that first lunge, you might be dead. If you manage to grab the audience from the outset, you have a good chance of holding onto them throughout the speech. But if you lose them at the beginning, you might as well just sit down.

The audience has *given* you their time. But their attention is something you have to *earn*. Whether you are a salesperson making a pitch for a new account or the CEO talking to the troops, you have to earn their interest. You can lead an audience to the speech, but you can't make them think. The only way you get them thinking and participating is to seize their attention. Otherwise, they'll shut down or shove off.

AN OPENING THAT SINGS

An executive of a major consumer products company was asked to welcome guests to his organization's 25th anniversary celebration.

When he reached the lectern he paused until there was absolute silence. Then he stunned the audience by singing:

Happy birthday to you,
Happy birthday to you,

Happy birthday dear (company name),
Happy birthday to you.

The audience was startled, thinking he may have taken leave of his senses. But their eyes were riveted to the speaker. He had their attention.

"Today is our 25th birthday," he went on to say. "Is that old for an organization? Young? Or are we in mid-life? Thank you all for being here and joining us in this look at where we've been, where we are, and where we're going."

He then went on to deliver an interesting, easy-to-follow dissertation on his company's beginnings, achievements, aspirations, and long-term aims.

He was daring. He was different. He was dramatic. And it worked.

THE COMPETITION

The minds of your audience are crowded with competing thoughts. You may have the podium, but the heads of your listeners are rattling with other matters. They are thinking about their:

- Jobs.
- Kids.
- Relationships.
- Financial stability.
- Health.
- Mortgages.
- Cars.

The start of the speech offers every listener the choice of heading down one of two roads. The first is to follow the speaker. The second is to ruminate over personal decisions, challenges, and worries, taking advantage of this free time to be self-absorbed.

You want your road to say "excitement" rather than "detour." Otherwise, you'll surely lose them.

A TOUCH OF DRAMA

Playwrights understand this well. In their films or stage productions, they'll do everything they can to immediately immerse you in their stories: a chase, a killing, a fight. Sometimes they're subtle; sometimes obvious; sometimes daring—but usually different.

You might remember this film: The scene opens on an empty veranda at a rubber plantation. Shots are fired off-camera. A man staggers onto the veranda, stumbles down a flight of stairs, and collapses.

This opening from the classic 1940 Bette Davis movie *The Letter* grabs your attention and won't let go. There is clear action, yet a sense of mystery about its meaning. It sets viewers' minds in motion trying to figure out the significance of the gunshots and death.

Here's an example of an excellent grabber from a speech given by the head of one of the world's leading transportation companies, who was concerned about his company's complacency. He began his speech to his top executives by listing former household-name companies no longer in business. Everyone took notice as his list grew longer and longer:

> The Packard Motor Car.
>
> Dumont TV's.
>
> Pan American World Airways.
>
> The Crosley.
>
> Eastern Air Lines.
>
> The Hudson.
>
> American Motors and the Nash Rambler.

> Just a few names of once-mighty U.S. companies now—in large part due to complacency—lying lifeless in a corporate graveyard. Could our company soon be lying next to them?

> Thank you all for coming today to hear me warn against the dangers—no, the plague—of complacency.

If that didn't get the attention of the executives in the audience, I'd be hard-pressed to suggest what would.

Of course, your opening can also be more traditional. A utility company executive was once asked to give a speech about which one of the two 1980 presidential candidates would be better for his industry. He began with:

> Carter? Reagan? For the utilities industry, which one? And why?
> Thank you for inviting me here this evening to assess which one of the two presidential hopefuls would be best for us in the energy-generating industry.

Note that in each of these two very different approaches, the presenter thanked the hosts, but not until after he knew he'd earned their attention. Avoid traditional "stock" beginnings. Aim to be bold. Seek to grab hold of the audience's attention.

TYPES OF GRABBERS

Questions are good grabbers. So are quotes. Personal observations and anecdotes work. Or you can start with a date as a prelude to a happening or event that might have an impact on your material.

Anecdotes

One very effective form of grabber is a story or anecdote. As we will discuss in the chapter on humor (Chapter 8), these can be somewhat tricky, but they are also a very effective way of drawing the listener into your tale. The best anecdotes are those that are not only entertaining but set up the key points of your speech. Consider this effective opening by Carole M. Howard of the Reader's Digest Association in a 1992 speech discussing lessons learned from their launch of magazine editions in Moscow and Budapest. She starts with a story:

> This past summer there was a story going around Moscow that the popular item at flea markets was a *used* light bulb. Yes, a used light bulb. Here's why:
> You buy a used light bulb for a few kopecks and take it to work. You then unscrew the good light bulb from your office lamp and replace it with the blown-out bulb. You tell your boss you need a new

light bulb because yours is out—and you take the original good bulb home. If you are lucky, you can also take the dead bulb home after it has been replaced, sell it at a flea market—and start the cycle all over again.

This story symbolizes for me what it's like to launch a new product in the former Soviet Union, now known as the Commonwealth of Independent States. On the one hand, you have consumers faced with horrendous shortages, endless lines, outrageous inflation, and a work force that doesn't seem very interested in working. On the other hand, however, you have an ingenuity and entrepreneurial spirit that even 70 years of communist domination could not completely crush.

This entrepreneurial spirit is even stronger in Hungary. . . .

During 1991, we launched two new editions of *Reader's Digest*—a Russian-language edition in July and a Hungarian edition in October—and set up operations in Moscow and Budapest. I am pleased to be asked to share our experiences with you.[2]

The beauty of the story is that not only is it interesting and pertinent, but it also illustrates the struggle between the challenges of scarce resources and the opportunities of entrepreneurship that are the themes of the speech. It is an intriguing and entertaining story, and it also makes a relevant point. Not only that, but it is set in the country that is the topic of discussion. It allows the speaker to grab the audience's attention and focus it squarely on the subject at hand.

Questions

The "Carter? Reagan?" opening described earlier in this chapter is a good example of a "question grabber." Question openings work because they challenge the listener to come up with an answer. The key is the question itself. It must be thought provoking and engage the listener's mind in coming up with an answer. It must also set the tone for the theme of the speech to follow.

One-Word Leads

One-word leads summarizing the topic work well and are a staple of broadcast news reporting. An example:

Plastics! Environmentalists say we can't get rid of them. I say we can.
Thank you all for inviting me here tonight to talk about . . .

Thematic Phrases

Thematic phrases are also effective here—at the top of your presentation—and repeated several times at key junctures throughout your delivery. The Reverend Jesse Jackson has used phrases
such as "keep hope alive" and "common ground" to tie together
his speeches and leave listeners with a resonating memory.

Powerful Statements or Dates

Profound and powerful statements will get attention. Roosevelt's
"December 7, 1941, is a day that will live in infamy," is an example of a profound and powerful statement. Lincoln's "four
score and seven years ago" is another example of using a "date"
as an opening.

Shocking Statistics

Shocking statistics and outrageous statements are each effective
grabbers:

Half the money spent on advertising is money thrown away.

Half of you will be dead within the next year. That's if we continue
to let the ozone layer dissipate.

Relate

The "relate" technique can be a good grabber. Here, you simply
inject yourself into the proceedings by relating to the previous
speaker or to the event occasioning your address. If you are part
of an extended program, it's a good idea to arrive early and listen
to as many preceding presenters as you can. This will enable you
to ferret out items in their material that can provide a bridge to
your own.

Case in point. Years ago, I was invited to address the annual meeting in Arizona of one of our nation's largest moving companies. The meeting was in Phoenix, and I was so backed up with appointments in New York the preceding day that I had to take the last flight out. That left me with at best three hours of sleep the night before I was scheduled to go on.

There is always a social component to these meetings, so I was not surprised when, in his opening remarks, the chairman referred to events on the golf course the previous day. He seemed to be getting some laughs about someone's green sneaker lost on the golf course.

Upon being introduced, I told everyone about my hectic day and late arrival, and asked if anyone had found my green sneaker on the golf course. The audience howled. From that moment on, I knew I had them.

My opening combined humor (with me being the butt of it) and the relate technique. It did the job.

The technique is simple. Merely use an idea, a phrase, or a word used by a previous speaker as a connector to your material. You can preferably use it in the beginning as a grabber. Or insert it at the appropriate time further along in your presentation.

As another example, Philadelphia Mayor Ed Rendell was introduced with a reference to a *Wall Street Journal* editorial commending his political courage and fearless decisions. He stepped up to the lectern and noted that there was actually a great deal of fear involved in his decisions. As for courage, he referred to John F. Kennedy, who, when asked how he became a war hero responded, "It was involuntary. They sank my boat." By tieing his opening into the introduction, he drew the audience in and had them laughing.

GOOD GRABBERS

The best grabbers are tailored to the specific speaker, audience, and occasion. Studying the effective grabbers of others can offer a model for generating your own. Here are a few of my favorites:

- John Paul Getty once told a group of would-be billionaires his secret of success: "Rise early, work hard, strike oil."
- Former Secretary of State Henry Kissinger once quipped, "At Harvard, it took me 10 years to achieve an environment of total hostility. Here in Washington, I've done it in just 20 months."
- "In the United States, optimism is perhaps our biggest export."
- John F. Kennedy: "I appreciate your welcome. And as the cow said to the Maine farmer, 'Thank you for a warm hand on a cold morning."
- Ronald Reagan: "It's morning again in America."
- British Prime Minister John Major: "No trade, no aid."
- On President Bush's record: "Four year ago, we were asked to read his lips. Now we can read his record."
- "On Wall Street, successful money managers buy the gloom and sell the boom."

WHATEVER IT TAKES

Whether you use any one of the techniques discussed in this chapter, opt for a song or pantomime, or shoot off fireworks, make sure your first point of contact with your listeners is designed to get their attention, while leading into the material that follows.

Chapter Checklist

Seize Their Attention

- If you do nothing else to prepare for your speech, make sure you have a good grabber. Start thinking about it when you first agree to give the speech.

- Memorize your grabber and deliver it looking straight at the audience. (For more on this, see the chapters in Part II, The Performance.)
- Can your speech start with:
  - An anecdote — "There is a story going around Moscow these days . . ."
  - A question — "Carter? Reagan? For the utilities industry, which one? And why?"
  - One-word lead — "Plastics! Environmentalist say we can't get rid of them."
  - Thematic phrase — "I have a dream."
  - Powerful statement — "December 7, 1941, is a day that will live in infamy."
  - Shocking statistic — "Half the money spent on advertising is thrown away."
  - Relate remark to prior speakers — "Has anyone seen my green sneaker?"

Death by Oratory

There is nothing worse than hearing a speaker start off by saying, "Can you all hear me back there?" You may be able to hear—but after that, you won't be listening.

- Don't start off slow and plan to build your way up. Start with a bang. The audience may not still be with you by the time you get rolling.
- Don't start with polite formalities. Save your "thank you" and "it is a privilege to address this distinguished audience" for after your grabber. These pleasantries are all expected and necessary but not exciting.
- Don't stoop just to get attention. Don't shout "sex" and when everyone looks up say, "now that I've got your attention, let me tell you what's really on my mind." Unless your talk happens to be about sex, stick to a grabber that relates to your subject matter.

Chapter Three

Give Them Road Maps and Signs

A small detachment from a Hungarian army unit was once lost during maneuvers in the Swiss Alps. It had snowed for two days, and the unit was all but given up for dead by the lieutenant who had dispatched them. But on the third day, the soldiers turned up at the base camp, safe and sound.

The lieutenant asked them how they had survived. The soldiers explained that they had at first despaired. But then one of them found a map in his pocket. That gave them hope. They pitched camp for two days and when the storm cleared, they used the map to discover their bearings.

The lieutenant looked at the map. He found that it was not a map of the Alps but a map of the Pyrenees. The soldiers had found their way back by following the *wrong* map![3] The map had so heartened and inspired them that they made the perilous trip back to camp. That was, perhaps, its most important function: It provided hope.

As this story illustrates, road maps can be important in inspiring and leading your troop of listeners through the unknown terrain of your talk. It is not important that you have the perfect road map. But it is important that you have a map.

A map gives your listeners hope. It allows them to look ahead and understand your goals. Many good ideas are wrapped in rambling presentations. Even well-organized speeches can miss their mark because the audience isn't able to grasp the direction quickly and easily.

Don't let your speeches stumble through a maze of muddled

ideas. Set them straight. Clothe them in clarity—and your audiences will bury you in blessings and ovations.

A road map gives listeners a structure that enables them to follow the speech. In addition, consider the echo effect: There's always a lag between the time the presenter articulates the words and the time they are received, absorbed, and processed by the listener. A lot of meaning falls through that gap, unless there is a road map to take the listener from one idea to the next.

You may know where you're going with your ideas. The audience doesn't. Helping them by previewing what's to follow ensures that they won't be developing any "concentration roadblocks." In the end, they might not accept your ideas. But they'll surely be able to follow them, and more than likely understand them.

For these reasons, it's essential that speakers provide the wherewithal for audiences to easily follow their thinking. In short, a speaker is not unlike a tour guide walking the group through some key messages.

SIGN LANGUAGE

Road maps provide the physical layout of your speech, the directions that move you from beginning to end, and the itinerary for stops along the way. At the start of the speech, the speaker is the only one with a clear sense of this overarching road map. The audience does not see the whole picture, but rather experiences the speech as a journey. It sees points along the way.

To make the road maps clear to the audience, speakers use a series of "signs," or transitions, that indicate what lies ahead and mark the progress along the route. Signs are strategically placed statements that meticulously lead listeners through your material. Imagine what it would be like riding on a superhighway and not knowing what's ahead until just before your exit, or, worse yet, just after your exit. Instead, what you see in most civilized societies is a series of signs leading up to the exit. "Two More

Miles!" and then "One More Mile!" and then "Get Off Right Here!"

Most of what we all learned about composition says that this series of signs is a redundancy that should be eliminated. Pare it back. Rout out that useless verbiage. One sign should be enough. People will lose interest if you keep telling them the same thing over and over.

But just as the driver on the superhighway has many distractions, so your listeners do also. Maybe they were distracted when you gave them the first road sign. Maybe they didn't care at that point. Maybe they just plain forgot what you said. So, as you complete each leg of your journey, you tell them, "This is where we have been. And this is what's still ahead." You need a clear roadmap for your speech, and you need to give your audience signs so they can follow it as well.

These signs, or transitions, are the threads that hold a presentation together. They are conveyor belts that smoothly move the audience from topic to topic. They are bridges between one topic or another.

SETTING THE SPEECH IN MOTION

The first sign is a complete description of your road map. This usually comes very close to the top of your talk, shortly after your grabber, and probably after you've taken care of housekeeping with the amenities and the thank-yous.

This is a critical juncture in your presentation. If your grabber worked, more than likely the audience is still with you, awaiting the next word. They'll even accept and tolerate your expressions of gratitude to your hosts as a necessary part of the proceedings. But if your next words aren't meaningful, your audience will more than likely find some train of thought that is easier to follow—namely, their own.

At this crucial crossroad, it's best to let people know where you're taking them so they'll know how to adjust their minds and they'll be more readily prepared to absorb the information flow.

This is like the road sign that has five or six destination points on it, nearest to farthest. This makes it clear where the journey is headed and provides a context for the later signs that deal with specific points along the way.

Today, I plan to discuss the social, economic, cultural, and political components of our new "Keep America Ahead" program.

This simple sign prepares people to focus on the four broad areas of the program you've just introduced:

- Social.
- Cultural.
- Economic.
- Political.

You now have an option. You've told the audience what's about to follow, so you can launch into your material by saying:

Let's first look at the social ramifications.

Or, you can take a step back before you launch into your four-point agenda by saying:

First, some background.

or

First, some perspective.

Here, you can discuss the origins of the Keep America Ahead program: Why it was created, how it evolved, how it will work, who will be affected, and why anyone should care.

By the way, three topics is probably the ideal number to cover in any given presentation. Audiences are comfortable with triads (yesterday, today, and tomorrow). Providing people with the topics you'd like them to follow also makes it easier on you. If you end up with more than three topics, try to pare them down or bundle a few of them together to create a neater package.

You've set your own course. Now all you have to do is navigate it.

Additional signs are called for as you move from topic to topic. Enter transitional statements, such as:

- So much for . . .   So much for economics. Now, let's turn to politics.
- Questions   We've discussed production, what about distribution?

  Where do we go from here?
- Emphatic statements   As for distribution, we've got the best system in the country.

These simple transitional statements alert the audience to the fact that you're moving on to the next agenda item you told them you planned to cover. This is the like the signs on the highway: "Thank you for visiting New York," or "Welcome to New Jersey. Please wear your safety belts."

Road maps and signs protect you against potential "tune outs." The audience will more than likely "tune in" because you cared enough about them to make it easier for them to go along with your thinking. The road map should be stated early on and where appropriate reinforced throughout the speech.

The map that is used can take many forms. In addition to the categories example of the Keep America Ahead program, there are many other possible structures for a speech. Let's examine them.

TYPES OF ROAD MAPS

There are as many different road maps as there are speeches. But there are several broad categories of road maps that are used to shape the structure of a speech. These include:

- Perspective.
- Definition.
- Problem solution and overview.
- Myth-Reality.

- Themes.
- Categories.
- Questions and rhetorical questions.

PERSPECTIVE ROAD MAP

The perspective road map permits presenters to take a step back and provide some historical background to any topic, any organization, any issue. From the podium, the road map of perspective sounds like this:

> Before proceeding, let's take a look at where we were, where we are, and ultimately, where we're going.

The long-range view it provides is especially useful because most of us focus on the short term. The peripheral vision approach offered by the frame of perspective enables people to see the wider scope, and it certainly makes it easier for them to absorb your ideas. It's simpler to accept a new direction (where we're going) when you appreciate the starting point (where we were).

DEFINITION ROAD MAP

The definition road map is especially useful when your organization is introducing a new product, service, system, or concept. It's useful because it allows the presenter to anticipate many of the questions arising out of such an introduction. The approach would go like this:

> Let me tell you what this new program is and:
> - When it will officially be introduced.
> - How it works, what it does, and how it does it.
> - Who it benefits, who it affects.
> - And what it means to you and why you should care.

The road map of definition allows you to address the most probable questions that will be asked about your new marketing direction, while satisfying the audience's curiosity in an organized, orderly, informative, and interesting way.

PROBLEM–SOLUTION OR OVERVIEW ROAD MAP

The problem-solution road map works when problems arise—a utility company outage; a strike; a fire; a burglary; a recall. Here, the overview scenario calls for you to answer three main questions:

- What the problem is.
- How we fixed it.
- The steps we've taken to make certain it never reoccurs.

Again, this format covers the gamut of concerns felt by many, if not all, of a presenter's constituents.

MYTH–REALITY ROAD MAP

The myth-reality road map comes in handy when you find yourself or your organization embroiled in controversy.

This map allows you to dispel erroneous information that may be circulating about you or your affiliation. It might sound something like this:

I'd like to clarify several myths circulating about recent events:

Myth: It has been suggested that we've been guilty of . . .
Fact: The facts are on our side . . .

Myth: We've been accused of . . .
Fact: The truth is . . .

Myth: Critics have wrongly implied we . . .
Fact: What we actually did . . .

THEME ROAD MAP

The theme road map serves to reinforce the focal point or key message of your presentation. Again, the classic theme frame is Martin Luther King's "I Have a Dream" speech. Strategically sprinkled throughout the presentation (but not overdone or over-worked) is the phrase "I Have a Dream," which reinforced Dr. King's vision for the future lives of African-Americans in this country. Such a theme may be repeated as many as six times in any given oration.

CATEGORIES ROAD MAP

The categories road map gives you a chance to fit your ideas into convenient slots. Example:

Today I plan to look at the three major components of the real estate market:
- Residential.
- Commercial.
- And industrial.

Having charted a course for yourself, it only remains for you to fill in the blanks using simple transition phrases.

QUESTION ROAD MAP

Finally, the question road map: Here again, you endeavor to ascertain the questions likely to surface on a given issue or development, then answer those questions up front.

Here's a sample of a question frame:

- When will we introduce our new technology?
- How much will it cost?

- Who are the potential buyers?
  Let's look.

A variation on this is the rhetorical question road map, in which you ask yourself one question at a time, then answer it before moving on to the next one.

I have heard that Lee Iacocca, when he was chairman of Chrysler, was given high marks for using the rhetorical question frame when some executives from his company were caught trying to pass off vehicles as new cars that had been driven several thousand miles and had their odometers turned back. At a press conference, Iacocca reportedly said:

Was that a dumb idea?
You bet it was.
Are we sorry it happened?
We sure are!
Is it going to happen again?
Not as long as I'm in this chair!

That was the end of a crisis that would have otherwise festered in the press and created even more problems for Chrysler. Iacocca took charge of the situation, admitted responsibility without dwelling on the problem, and promised to take action to rectify it.

IN CONCLUSION . . .

There's an old journalism saying that suggests writers "tell them what you're going to tell them, tell them, then tell them what you told them." This repeating of the central themes of the speech is one of the key functions of road maps and signs. Tell them early, and tell them often.

When your speech is drafted, go through it with a "sign crew" and make sure all the transitions are clearly marked. Make sure you tell your listeners up front about the road map you intend to use and then give them signs at key points along the way. This will ensure they won't get lost. And they just might be willing to follow you almost anywhere.

Give Them Road Maps and Signs

- Does your speech provide a well-organized road map for the audience to follow?
- Do you describe the framework shortly after your grabber?
- Do you use transition phrases and other signs to move from one topic to the next?
- In designing your speech, try using one of the following road maps:
  - Perspective   Past, present, and future.
  - Definition   Let me tell you what this is . . .
  - Problem-solution   Here's what's wrong. Here's how we fixed it.
  - Myth-reality   People believe this about us. Fact: It isn't true. Here's why.
  - Theme   I have a dream.
  - Categories   Today, I plan to look at three major components of the real estate market.
  - Question   When will we introduce our new technology?
- Does your conclusion sum up and reinforce your road map?

Death by Oratory

The speaker had them all on the edge of their seats. He was deftly reeling off words, dazzling them with his wit and charm. But when the speech was over, everyone scratched their heads and asked: What was the point? They had enjoyed the tour, but they had no idea where they had been, because he hadn't given them a road map.

- Don't expect listeners to find their own way through your speech or think that brilliance will make up for lack of order. Have a map and stick to it.
- Don't start off saying you are going to cover 10 items and only cover 7.
- Don't take your travelers to more than three destinations in one trip, if you can help it. You might get away with a 10-point itinerary if the stops are short and clearly connected—but three is ideal.
- Don't leave listeners hanging at the end of the speech. Tell them where they have been. They will appreciate the recap.

Chapter Four

The Conclusion
Go Out in Style

There are many interesting ways to signal that you have reached the end of your speech. You could have a fat lady sing. Porky Pig could stroll out and stutter "That's All Folks!" Or you could suddenly pick up your hat and coat and dash away from the podium. There are more graceful ways to make an exit.

Many speakers signal that they have reached the end of their speech by saying "Thank you" or, more formally, "Ladies and Gentlemen, I thank you very much for your kind attention." It gets the job done, but not much more.

If you feel like you have to conclude your speech with a thank-you just to let people know you are finished, then you haven't written a strong conclusion. I am all for politeness—there is little enough left of social graces these days—but to finish a speech with the words "Thank you" is as deadly as it is delicate.

You want to reach a point where your audience is thanking you for the opportunity to listen. That comes with a strong speech and a strong conclusion. If, in the meantime, you feel the need to thank your audience, by all means, do so. But write a speech that doesn't require a thank you. To do that, you need to clearly signal that you have reached your conclusion.

If you end with "thank you," you may also be missing a great opportunity. It is like running a commercial for a cure for baldness without flashing up the toll-free number. ("Well, that's our marvelous new cure. Thank you for your attention.") Even if what you are selling is a little more lofty than a hair-growth formula—even if you are not selling anything—you still need to close with a direct appeal to your listeners.

A fundamental mistake in sales is to walk away without "asking for the order." It is the same in speechmaking. How many brilliant speeches build up a tremendous amount of interest and goodwill, only to let it dissipate in a weak conclusion? You've got their attention, you've made your case. This is the place to make an impact.

This appeal could be an emotional one. It could be a challenge. Or it could make your audience want to do something. Or change their thinking about a subject. Whatever the purpose, it should harness the power of all the words that came before it and focus this energy on a single goal.

SUMMING UP

Before the appeal, the conclusion should sum up where you have been in the speech and reinforce any conclusions you have drawn along the way. It is an opportunity to reshape and clarify the information you have presented. Your listeners have probably already forgotten what went on at the opening of the speech. It is your job to remind them. Refer back to your grabber if you can. Tie together the key points of the speech.

But don't just rattle off a list of points. Pull them together into a form that makes more sense of them. For example, suppose you started out with a category frame:

Today I plan to look at three major components of the real estate market:
- Residential.
- Commercial.
- And industrial.

Your conclusion could examine common elements of all three markets:

As we have seen, all three segments of the real estate market are in a downturn. Residential markets are down. Commercial are down. Industrial are down. But that doesn't mean you have to be down.

The commercial markets, at least in our area, show the most promise in the immediate future. If I were going to invest in real estate, that would be where I'd put my money. So, proceed with caution. But for those with the vision and skill to find winners, there are still plenty of opportunities for profits.

This summing up may not always be as formal as the above example. Sometimes, it can be as simple as restating the opening theme or grabber of the speech, with a slight twist. This can be an effective way of bringing the speech full circle. John F. Kennedy, in his famous "Ich Bin Ein Berliner" speech, concludes by referring back to his opening:

All free men, wherever they may live, are citizens of Berlin, and, therefore, as a free man, I take pride in the words "Ich bin ein Berliner."[4]

Adlai Stevenson, speaking on the future of American cities, concluded the speech with a statement of his hope for the future: "Thus will we build and rebuild our cities, and in so doing renew and rekindle our faith in ourselves and in the limitless creativeness of free men."[5] He summarizes his theme of rebuilding the cities, and then moves to the larger theme of the "limitless creativeness of free men." Moving from the small to the large is a good way to conclude a speech.

CUT TO THE QUICK

You might want to precede your summary with a short statement such as: "So what I'm saying here today is . . ." or "As we have seen . . ." Once you give the signal that you are nearing your conclusion, however, tie things up as quickly as possible.

Words such as *finally* or *in conclusion* or *in closing* seem to release a hormone in the bodies of listeners. Within a minute or two, the adrenaline begins to flow. Once this hormone is released, listeners need either to direct this energy into a hearty applause or work it off in impatient foot tapping and fidgeting. There is nothing worse than a speech that appears to be reaching its conclusion and then drones on minute after minute. It is like the frustration of being in a car two blocks from your destination and finding all the streets run one way in the wrong direction. You end up driving far without going anywhere.

Once you sum up, then you need to arrive at some kind of direct appeal or conclusion. Sometimes this can be done all in one sentence, as in the case of Kennedy's Berlin speech or Stevenson's speech on cities. But other times, you want to make a more specific appeal or spend a few sentences on it.

PASSION AND HOPE

The conclusion can be a crescendo, where the entire orchestra is playing passionately. It is designed not to move the audience to a specific action but to move their hearts.

Jesse Jackson concluded his speech to the 1992 Democratic Convention with a story about a pair of twins—"a dwarf and a giant"—a sister and brother he met on a southern college campus. The "giant" had been offered athletic scholarships around the country but had turned them down to stay with his sister and look out for her.

Jackson concludes:

> Not all of us can be born tall, some are born short, motherless, abandoned, hungry, orphaned. Somebody has to care. It must be us. And if we do, we will win, and deserve to win.
> Keep hope alive.

To move the audience, the conclusion to the speech sometimes has little connection to the themes that went before. In Jesse Jackson's speech, his closing story and statement related back to themes of caring and hope that he had introduced earlier.

Martin Luther King's most famous speech also ends with a statement of hope:

> [W]e will be able to speed up that day when all of God's children, black men and white men, Jews and Gentiles, Protestants and Catholics, will be able to join hands and sing in the words of the old Negro spiritual, "Free at last! Free at last! Thank God almighty, we are free at last!"[6]

This closing draws together King's earlier comments on unity and justice, but moves them forward. He could have ended with a reference back to his "I have a dream" theme or the "let freedom ring" theme that followed it. But, instead, he uses the conclusion to draw together and extend these two themes.

In his closing, King describes his dream for the end of ethnic and religious division as if it were reality. He doesn't express the wish of "Let freedom ring" but rather the realization of "free at last!"

Summarizing and extending your themes is tricky to do, and not every speech lends itself to this kind of treatment. But it can be a very effective way of concluding, without specifically ticking off each of the major themes you presented. King's closing also shows how much art is involved in an effective conclusion.

General Douglas MacArthur used a reference to a very different kind of song to end his famous speech to the Joint Session of Congress on April 19, 1951. His remarks dealt with his reasons for urging an all-out war in Korea, a stand that led to conflicts with President Harry Truman and MacArthur's dismissal as leader of the U.S. and U.N. armed forces. MacArthur makes specific recommendations in the speech, but instead of closing with a call to action, he ends with an emotional farewell. This may have been the wisest course, in that he had little hope of actually reversing national policy. This ending added immeasurably to the emotional appeal of the speech. Many eyes were moist when he concluded.

He didn't say, "Given these considerations, inaction is more dangerous than action. I urge the members of the Senate and House to move decisively to pressure the president to change his policy in the region. To support the courageous Korean people. And to stand against the communist aggressors. This is the true test of our commitment to democracy and freedom."

Instead, he ended with words that the nation will never forget for their power, emotion, and simplicity. In closing, he referred to the lyrics of an old military ballad that said, "old soldiers never die; they just fade away."

And, like the old soldier of that ballad, I now close my military career and just fade away, an old soldier who tried to do his duty as God gave him the light to see that duty. Goodbye.[7]

His ending arguably might have been more direct and specific. But it is hard to imagine that it could have been more moving. Unlike King's battle cry, this is a swan song. It is perhaps an irony that the pacifist Dr. King ended with such forceful words while the warrior MacArthur left the podium so softly. Both approaches were effective—one designed to call people to action, the other designed, it seems, to explain MacArthur's position and reshape his image as a warmonger.

If you want to move your audience, to reach their hearts, be sure to end with an emotional appeal of some kind. This could be a story, a song, a quote, a statement of hope, or a vision for the future. Not all speeches, particularly in business, lend themselves to this kind of denouement. You may want to leave them with a question or other challenge or urge them to take more specific actions.

CHALLENGE

Sometimes, the speaker leaves listeners with a challenge, questions to chew on. This closing is designed to challenge the audience to think but not necessarily tell them how to think. Your speech may have suggested your opinion on the issue, but here, you are asking for your listeners to shape their own responses.

Toward the end of a speech to *Reader's Digest* global editors, George V. Grune, chairman and chief executive officer of the Reader's Digest Association, rattled off a series of questions:

I've tried to describe just how much power you have to affect the success of your own edition (of the magazine), the global magazine, and the entire company.

Now, what will you do with that power?

In what new ways will you inform, educate, inspire, and entertain?

How will you keep *Reader's Digest* one step ahead of the competition, locally and globally?

What will you do to attract the best writers and seek out cutting-edge articles?

How will you combat media fragmentation?

How many new customers will you bring through our front door?

What will you contribute to increased advertising sales, higher circulation, increased renewal percentages, and improved newsstand sales?

Grune continued with several more questions. He then concluded with a call to action. He read a letter from a young U.S. soldier in the Persian Gulf (during the Persian Gulf War) stating how much the soldier relied on the magazine for hope. Then, he concluded:

> That is the power of a great magazine! In so many ways, we are depending on you to increase that power—now and into the 21st century—so we will be an even greater magazine and an even greater company.
> The power is in your hands.[8]

PERSUASION: CALL TO ACTION

Some closings call listeners to specific action. Hire our company. Buy our product. Write your legislators to oppose this pending law. Improve your service. Paul Revere's speech was short but highly effective: "To arms. To arms." The conclusion can be where you call for action or ask for the sale.

In a speech to employees, Robert Baer, CEO of United Van Lines, sums up by reinforcing his message on the importance of customer service. He had opened his remarks by reading complaint letters from customers. He concluded by reading positive letters, and then this closing paragraph:

> So what does all of this mean? One thing is certain: Sharply contradictory customer views of our service should cause all of us to take notice and take corrective action. But at the same time United has reason for optimism, and the picture is far from gloomy. In my view, we can and will retain our momentum if we concentrate on doing, not talking. . . . If we take planned, calculated action, rather than reflexive reaction; if we recognize that no competitive advantage lasts

very long. . . . When you get down to it, the United difference is dependent, not on the wheel of fortune, but on each one of us.[9]

He urged his employees to improve the service they deliver to customers. His clear message with its clear call for action had greater impact since it was wrapped in an emotional appeal.

If you are making a corporate presentation on your product, you will probably want to end by asking for a sale. If you are speaking to potential customers or supporters outside of a sales presentation, you can still make a request, but not a direct one. If you are a consultant, you might talk about the challenges companies face and the importance of sound advice. You could use the opportunity to relate some of your successes, ostensibly to illustrate a point in your speech, but also to show the audience that you are effective in your work.

Chapter Checklist

The Conclusion

- Have you summarized the key points in your speech at the closing?
- If possible, have you referred back to your grabber and opening?
- Can you touch on broader implications of your comments?
- Have you extended your themes to inspire your audience, challenge them, or urge them to action?
- Have you "asked for the sale"?

Death by Oratory

Well, that's all I have to say. Thank you.

I think I've covered everything (looking down at a notecard). Yes, that's all. Thank you very much for your attention.

Avoid this type of ending. Also:

- Don't leave without asking for the sale.
- Don't expect your ending to fall into place. Even if you haven't written out text for the whole speech, make sure you know exactly what you are going to say at the conclusion.
- Don't end on a low or indecisive note. End with a crescendo that will draw people out of their seats.
- Don't stray too far from your theme at the end. Don't introduce new topics of discussion or launch into a new area. Sum up where you've been and give it slightly broader emphasis.
- Don't act like you are going to end the speech and then drone on and on and on. It could provoke a riot.

TEXTURE

Like great art and beautiful music, a good speech has texture. You have the framework for a great speech: A snappy grabber, a clear road map, and a dynamic conclusion. But the impression you make depends on what you paint on this canvas.

Texture is the character of the speech. It is a combination of ingredients that create the "feel" of the speech. The grabber sets the tone for the speech in addition to providing an opening. But after that, texture comes from the threads that are woven together in the speech: the sounds of words, visual images, personal involvement and stories, humor, and numbers. Texture is created by the interaction between the speaker and the audience.

Chapter Five

Write for the Ear

"It's morning time in America. From the outhouse to the courthouse to the state house to the White House, it's morning time in America."

Jesse Jackson

A braham Lincoln, who had a finely developed ear for the spoken word, used to drive his law partner crazy by reading books and articles aloud in their office in Springfield, Illinois. He would read aloud from Shakespeare's plays to anyone who would listen (and some who wouldn't). Lincoln felt that listening to the spoken word sharpened his ear.

We can hear this sharp ear in Lincoln's phrases such as "The ballot is stronger than the bullet" or "Let us have faith that right makes might, and in that faith let us to the end dare to do our duty as we understand it."

A speech is more than ideas. It is sound! It is music! It is rhythm! It is rhyme! It is poetry! It is performance! Focusing on the ideas alone is like trying to sell a car without a paint job. It is the shimmer of the paint that attracts buyers as much as what's under the hood.

Mark Twain, whose ear was as finely tuned as his sense of humor, once observed that the difference between the correct word and the nearly correct word is like the difference between lightning and a lightning bug. Finding the right words can give your speech a spark.

When you're preparing your presentation, it is essential to focus on the way it will sound, as opposed to the way it will read.

In this age of "sound bites," we are more aware than ever of the need to turn a captivating and unforgettable phase. Even if the television cameras and microphones are not in the audience when you deliver your speech, the brilliantly worded phrases will be what resonate in the ears of your listeners after they leave.

In President Clinton's 1993 inaugural address, he used the phrase "There is nothing wrong with America that cannot be cured by what is right with America." It was one of those phrases that resonated in the minds of listeners, and it was picked up as a sound bite for news broadcasts on the event.

"Ear appeal" phrases can be like the haunting songs of a musical that the members of the audience find themselves humming on the way home. Even if people want to forget them, they can't.

A good ear appeal phrase compels the listener to not only remember it but also repeat it. Word of mouth, marketers tell us, is still one of the most powerful influences impacting receptivity. A phrase that's heard, that makes such an impression on the listener that it's repeated over and over, is a phrase with ear appeal. It should have a sense of mystery and drama in it—enough mystery so that listeners are intrigued but not so much that they are confused.

Examples of such phrases include:

- We have nothing to fear but fear itself.
- Read my lips.
- You're the right one, baby.
- No pain, no gain.
- It ain't over till it's over.

Speechgivers should strive to have lots of ear-appealing phrases in each presentation. The following methods should help you come up with them.

RHYMES, ALLITERATION, AND SOUND-ALIKES

Rhymes, alliteration, and sound-alikes are memorable because words that sound similar are easy to recall.

- What we need are jobs, not barbs.
- The homeless are not helpless.
- He was both amusing and amazing.

The words *homeless* and *helpless* sound alike. They make the listener pay attention to them—they leave an impression. Once listeners are captivated by an ear appeal phrase, they're likely to pay attention to the rest of your material.

Rhyming words can also be effective, if they are not overused. Consider the following:

- Will the surge in the urge to merge continue? Or is the current trend too hot not to cool down?

Alliteration—using words that start with the same sound—adds to ear appeal. Examples:

- Both merchants and Muslims alike abhor the occupation.
- If you rest, you rust.

PARALLEL PHRASES

Parallel phrases evoke powerful images and also help snare the listener's interest. When the Reverend Jesse Jackson suggested he was going to take his movement from the outhouse to the courthouse to the state house to the White House (see the chapter opening quote), audiences roared. The words played off each other and were Jackson's rallying cry.

And consider this closing from a 1991 speech by Christine D. Keen, a manager at the Society for Human Resource Management:

> As a country, we're at a point where we need to choose between the barbarians and the bureaucrats, between patching up the existing institutions of the industrial era and creating new institutions for the new era.[10]

Juxtaposing words that sound similar is another effective tool to impact the ear. Even using the same word twice can set up parallel phrases that can be used to create a subtle twist in logic. This twist helps keep listeners involved, while furthering the point of the speech. Cases in point:

I'd rather feed the Russians now than fight the Russians later.

The credit crunch has as much to do with the economy as Captain Crunch.

The president is more interested in events in the Mideast than the economics of the Midwest.

This structure provides a sharp contrast between the concepts that are parallel—*feed* versus *fight*, or world events versus the domestic economy. It also can be used to ridicule an accepted concept such as the credit crunch by reducing it to Captain Crunch.

CONTRASTING PHRASES

In addition to parallel phrases, another way to highlight the contrast between two ideas is to use directly contrasting words and phrases.

I wish the president had seen the light. Unfortunately, I think he's just felt the heat.

The one-syllable words *light* and *heat* contrast nicely and remain with the listener.

Opposing prepositions can set the table for a powerful statement that remains in the listener's ear.

Voters may forget what you did *for* them, but they'll rarely forgive you for what you did *to* them.

Here, the words *forget* and *forgive* play well off each other, as do the prepositions *for* and *to*.

RECURRENT THEMES

As we examined in Chapter 3, a recurrent theme can help organize a speech. If the words of that theme are chosen carefully, it can also leave a lasting impression. Words such as "keep hope alive" or "I have been to the mountaintop" live in the mind, the ear, and the heart long after the speech is concluded.

ADAPT STREET SLANG OR SLOGANS

Street slang can offer direct and striking language that can wake up your listeners. An executive speaking about the need for fewer government regulations might say: "I implore the EPA to cut us some slack." The danger of slang is that it can interrupt the tone of the speech. For example, George Bush's handlers debated whether to include the street-tough phrase "read my lips" in his speech because it was considered unpresidential.

This danger is also the power of using slang and slogans. Another risk is that eventually popularized phrases outlive their timeliness. "The mother of all . . ." (patterned after Saddam Hussein's description of the Persian Gulf War as the "Mother of All Battles") is one example of a popularized phrase that has had its day in the sun. "Read my lips" is probably another.

CREATING WORDS

Finally, one way to affect the ear is to create your own word:

- Trans capitalization.
- Logo cop.
- Synchron totality.

Words you create can be fun. They can be memorable. But to truly make sure they're understood, you'll probably have to spend some time defining them.

TUNING UP YOUR PHRASES

Even if you are not adept at turning out ear-catching phrases, you can increase the ear appeal of your remarks by some fairly simple fine-tuning. Sometimes, even minor changes can have a major effect on the impact of a speech.

One powerful way to gain ear appeal is to delete prepositions and connector phrases to break thoughts into short sentences. For example, instead of:

He changed her looks and he changed her life.

simply say:

He changed her looks. He changed her life.

By deleting the word *and*, you strengthen the statement and make it easier for your audience to follow. Breaking two thoughts into two sentences adds rhythm to any presentation—it also varies the pace while heightening understanding, providing an audibly interesting way for audiences to follow your thinking.

The best way to tune your ear is to listen to the spoken word. Listening to speeches, reading poetry aloud, or even reading text aloud, and listening, can give you a better feel for the effects of the sounds of words. Another good place to observe ear appeal is in broadcast news shows where you'll hear such statements as

America has too many financiers and not enough engineers.

Be sure to factor the ear into the preparation and presentation of your next speech.

KEEP IT SIMPLE

To me, the essence of good communications has always been simplicity. I prefer one-syllable words to fancier ones. Otherwise, you're talking down to the audience. To me, it's a matter of caring enough about the audience to make it easy for them to follow your reasoning.

That's why, unless you're giving a highly technical, highly scientific presentation in engineering or medical terms, opt for a conversational tone. Pretend your audience is composed of people you might run into at a cocktail party who ask you for your thoughts on a topic of mutual concern.

Should you find yourself with no other option than to use multisyllabic words, it's a good technique to immediately define the terms you use in case some members of the audience are unfamiliar with them. Immediately following your use of an uncommon or very technical term, you might add, "By that, of course, I mean . . ."

The easier you make it for your audience, the more appreciative they're likely to be and the more receptive they're likely to become.

In sum, be conversational.

Chapter Checklist

Write for the Ear

- Can you add phrases that contribute to the ear appeal of your speech?
- Can you tune up your text to increase its ear appeal?
- Can you use the following techniques?
  - Rhymes, alliteration, and sound-alikes.
  - Parallel phrases.
  - Contrasting phrases.
  - Recurrent themes.
- Does your speech use popularized phrases that should be cut?

Death by Oratory

A professor with a grand idea wrapped it up and supported it with qualifications and large, cumbersome words. The argument was brilliant but the audience didn't hear it. It never got past their ears to their minds. If the professor had clothed the idea in more appealing language, it might have had a greater effect.

- Don't use the first words that come to your mind. Instead, say the words aloud and listen to them. Try alternatives to see how they sound. Find the best sound that communicates your idea.

- Don't think that because you are clear, you will have impact. Clarity is not what makes an impact on the listener, although it helps. Ear appeal equals impact.

- Don't sound like a scientist or a lawyer, even if you are one. Use words that are clear and melodious.

Chapter Six

Eye Appeal
Show Them What You Mean

C an you see a speech? One might argue that the eye has no role to play in the development and delivery of a speech. This view may be myopic. Your ability to weave a tale, to call up forceful images in the minds of the audience, is crucial to keeping their attention and reaching them. If you show them effective imagery, they will *see* your point.

Images linger and work their way into the listener's consciousness and even vocabulary. Churchill's description of a communist "Iron Curtain" was such a powerful image that it survived throughout the Cold War.

Your speech, like a story, is a canvas on which you can write many words or paint pictures. Words are more easily forgotten than images. Images tend to appeal more directly to the mind and stick with the listener. So use your words as much as possible to paint pictures.

If a picture is worth a thousand words, you can see what an economical use of language it is to use a few dozen words to paint a picture.

Personal stories can be an important way to appeal to the mind's eye, as we will discuss in Chapter 7. Direct stories about yourself or others can provide concrete images for audiences to take in. But there are also other ways to appeal to the mind's eye, particularly through imagery.

IMAGERY

During his inaugural address, President Clinton spoke of meeting in "the depth of winter," but "by the words we speak and the faces we show the world, we force the spring."

Properly used, these images paint unforgettable and understandable pictures for listeners who may not be able to follow a torrent of complex details about the economy, but they do understand winter and spring. Simple, graphic imagery can give them something that is easy to grasp.

Imagery is also a powerful sword. As Clinton used imagery, so it was turned against him on the campaign trail. Texas Senator Phil Gramm described then presidential candidate Clinton this way:

> At the New York convention, Clinton was like a used car salesman peddling his vehicle for change. The wax job was shiny. The hubcaps sparkled. The upholstery was spotless. The paint was new. But when you look under the hood, he was peddling a model from the '70s—a Carter-mobile with the axle broken and frame bent to the left.

In addition to using imagery to attack opponents, speakers also use imagery to teach the audience about complex issues. When Senator Gramm was asked why everyone should have to pay for the savings and loan bailout when most of the financial institutions involved are located in the West and Southwest, he answered metaphorically:

> The train wreck may have taken place in the West and the Southwest, but the passengers—the depositors—were from all over the country. That's why people from all over the country will have to pay.

Imagery can also give your audience an intuitive feel for a situation. Consider, for example, this passage from a speech by Marilyn Pred, director of public relations for Omaha Steaks International, in discussing building a positive corporate image:

> An image is built over the years, like a house, brick by brick. But it can be demolished with one swing of the wrecking ball.[11]

Caution: Overdosing on Imagery

On the other hand, images can become so vague that they become meaningless. There is a scene in the Peter Sellers movie *Being There* in which his artless musings about gardening are seen as prophetic analogies for the economic struggles of the nation. But these analogies were not a sign of sage wisdom but rather a bumbling lack of wisdom. Speakers who string together analogy after analogy may make themselves perfectly clear, but come off as shallow.

Because images are so powerful, they should be saved for choice points in the speech. The ideal use of imagery is to highlight your key points at the opening of a speech. This ensures that the image will remain fixed in the minds of the listeners throughout the speech. It also means you will have plenty of time to flesh the image out. And your audience will remember the part of the speech that you want them to remember, rather than some beautiful segment of the speech that is tangential to your main points.

BOMBSHELLS AND WEASEL WORDS

Words, themselves, often evoke strong emotional reactions from the audience. They can paint a halo above your subject or cast a dark cloud over it. They can be a bombshell that is provocative or help to calm and deflect controversy.

What's in a name? A rose by any other name might be called a *weed* instead of a *flower*. Obviously, the former is far less flattering than the latter. Similarly, a violinist could be called a fiddler or a virtuoso. When the United Parcel Service (UPS) in its advertising compared competition in the package industry to the "arms race," it made it clear that it meant business.

As one veteran political activist suggested, language doesn't just shape a campaign, it *is* the campaign.

Words can be lethal. In warfare, derogatory nicknames are often used to dehumanize the enemy soldiers to make it possible to kill them. When President George Bush compared the actions of Saddam Hussein to Hitler, it gave the Gulf War a moral imperative. Similarly, Bosnian Serbs used the chilling term *ethnic cleansing* in a feeble attempt to mask the cruelty of their campaign against Bosnian Muslims. Others compared the actions to the *Holocaust*, using charged words to reinforce their views.

Minority groups are particularly sensitive about the choice of language. For example, gay and lesbian groups take issue with terms such as *sexual preference* because it implies the individual has a choice. They prefer using, instead, *sexual orientation*. Similarly, they are concerned by the phrase *acknowledged homosexual*, which sounds like the person is admitting to a criminal offense, or the phrase *homosexual lifestyle*, which to some evokes images of drag queens and freak shows.

The associations of certain words also change over time. For example, the term *Negro* eventually became so tainted with negative overtones that it was replaced by *black* and, more recently, by *African-American*. It is important to keep up with current usage.

Many speakers are tempted to use "weasel words" to try to reshape reality. These range from fairly innocuous euphemisms such as *he passed away* instead of *he died* to more devious twists of language such as calling nuclear missiles *peacekeepers*. When companies call layoffs *strategic reductions in force* or *downsizing*, it may seem to take the edge off the personal tragedy involved in the process, but no one is fooled.

Some of these attempts to rename reality are such transparent frauds that they do more to undermine the credibility of the speaker than change the perception of the listener. The "Ministry of Truth" in George Orwell's *Nineteen Eighty-Four* may have been able to get away with such nonsense, but the choice of words alone can rarely transform a Mr. Hyde into a Dr. Jekyll. Words can change the lighting on your subject, but they cannot turn a devil into an angel.

So, choose your words wisely. Words can build up your subject or tear it down. Weigh your words carefully, because "a rose by any other name" will *not* smell as sweet.

THE REAL EYES

In addition to engaging the mind's eye, there are sometimes opportunities to appeal to the actual eyes of the audience. When President Reagan wanted to show how complex the federal budget had become, he brought in the huge document to hold up during his speech. The CEO of one company would shock new sales recruits when he ended his pep talk by plunging a combat knife into a beach ball emblazoned with the name of the company's rival. This kind of stunt is certainly not for the faint of heart, but it offers a dramatic impact that goes beyond what could be achieved by words alone.

Even when you have less shocking statements to make, you might bring in other props to help you illustrate your points. They provide visual interest and relief during the speech.

The most common appeal to the eye is audiovisuals. These can offer very effective ways of engaging the audience. We will discuss more about their uses and abuses in Chapter 10.

Chapter Checklist

Eye Appeal

- What parts of your speech will appeal to the mind's eye of the audience?
- Where can you add images to your speech?
- Do you have too many images without enough substance to back them up, flesh them out, and make them real?
- Is there an image (such as the coming of spring) that can be used to sum up your main point?

Death by Oratory

A three-ring circus is not a good model for a speech. If there are too many activities going on, no matter how good you are at being ringmaster, your poor audience will succumb to sensory overload. This is not a bad thing to happen at a circus, but it is deadly for a speech. So if you are talking in one ring, holding up props, and flashing overheads on a screen, you may be trying to do too much. A speech should appeal to the ears and eyes, but not overwhelm them.

- Don't load too much imagery into the speech. One beautiful image after another may take your audience on a delightful ride but leave them with little when they finish.

- Don't mix images. If you are talking about fish in the ocean and then shift to a discussion of birds of a feather you may end up with a speech that is neither fish nor fowl. Find a good image and stick with it.

- Avoid tired metaphors. Even "springtime" is a bit overused. Ask yourself, can you see this image in your own mind as you say it, or is it worn out?

Chapter Seven

Put Yourself into the Speech

I 've been told that in Japan it's considered rude for one to talk about oneself. (That may be why we have a best-selling auto-biography called *Iacocca* but no comparable one called *Morita*.) But if you are going to speak, and speak about what you know, then be prepared to talk about yourself and your own experiences.

At the 1992 Democratic National Convention, Jesse Jackson spoke about the plight of the working poor—not in statistics or broad terms but in specific stories from the front lines. He told about going to Hamlet, North Carolina, where 25 workers died in a chicken factory fire after owners had locked the doors from the outside. He said:

> The workers died trapped by economic desperation and oppressive work laws. One woman came up to me after the fire—she said "I want to work. I don't want to go on welfare. I have three children and no husband. We pluck 90 wings a minute. Now I can't bend my wrist, I got the carpel thing. Then when we're hurt they fire us, and we have no health insurance, and no union to help us. . . ." If we keep Hamlet in our hearts and before our eyes, we will act to em-power working people.

This is much more powerful than if he had talked about statistics on the number of workers who don't have medical insurance or spoke generally about the challenges facing poor Americans. It is even more effective than if he had related a story he had read in the newspaper. The story is direct because it is personal, pow-erful, credible. It draws the listener into the event.

A good speech contains many firsthand observations and accounts. That's what makes it believable. That's what makes it human.

Don't be shy about using the personal pronoun *I*. Tell it through your eyes. Tell it through the eyes of people you've met and observed. Tell anecdotes about the events and changes you've seen and the people behind them.

But a caution against overworking the personal pronouns, for they might make you appear too possessive, too conceited. Strike a happy balance, and your personalized experiences should heighten receptivity of your material. In other words, it's OK to use the pronoun *I*, but not the pronoun *my*.

The key word here is balance, a mixture of what you see and say, what people on the scene have witnessed and what others can favorably attest to when it comes to the work you're doing. What we're talking about is "personalization."

Steven Rosenzweig, president of Concorde, Inc., a Philadelphia-based health-care management company, used a personal story in a 1991 speech to an Illinois trade association to drive home the point that companies can take action to control their rising health-care costs.

Back in July, I conducted an unintentional experiment in managing health-care costs. I fell down the stairs at home. I walked around in pain for a couple of days until one of our nurses convinced me to see a doctor. The fifth metatarsal in my right foot was broken. So I went to see our orthopedic surgeon. He told me I would be in a cast with crutches for 6 to 8 weeks. Then I would probably need another 6 to 8 weeks of physical therapy.

I wasn't about to be out of work for more than a month because of a foot. Two days later, I told my doctor to take the cast off or I would saw it off in my garage. He reluctantly agreed to take off the cast. I bought myself a walking cast and a cane and kept working. By the second week, I was just using the cane. By the third week, I had dropped the cane. By the fourth week, I was walking all over Europe with my family on vacation. I've been X-rayed and I'm fine. I have been able to dance all the way to the bank.

If I had gone the route the physician recommended, my fall would have cost me and the company thousands of dollars in medical benefits and lost time. Instead, my total bill was for a $230 cast, a few

X-rays and a couple of visits to the doctor. How does this happen? Because no one is watching the store.

He then launched into an explanation of some of the current problems of corporate health-care management and some of the ways companies can combat rising costs. The interesting, well-presented personal anecdote helped demonstrate some of the flaws of the system and show how a motivated employer can work around them. He even brought his crutches and walking cast along as a prop.

Rosenzweig also referred to the incident at the close of the speech, telling the executives that, "Like my foot, your business doesn't need to be bound up by heavy health-care costs. You can cut through them. You will be happier and your employees will be healthier. And you will be able to dance all the way to bank."

Personalization also allows you to talk about specifics rather than empty generalizations. Instead of talking about the extensive research and field tests your organization has done, use specific examples to show it. Talk about the field tests you personally were involved in at Farmer Brown's dairy farm in Wisconsin, where Farmer Brown reports that as a result of using the new hormone developed by your company, his cows now yield twice the normal amount of milk at half the feeding cost.

> After spending a week with the Browns, getting up day after day for the 5:00 A.M. milking and watching the family change from skeptics to believers, I—and they—are convinced this new hormone is commercially feasible.

HUMANIZE

In addition to your own firsthand accounts, you can also tell stories about others.

Which of these two excerpts from speeches is more interesting?

1. Health-care costs are soaring. If they continue to escalate at the current rate of 10 percent per year, many small businesses will be strangled and will not survive.

2. The sign outside the auto repair shop reads "Dino and Artie's. Fixing your transmissions since 1945." Dino Eviginedes and Artie Messina are World War II veterans who survived the assault on Iwo Jima. They have lasted through the ups and down of more than 40 years of running a small business. They are fighters. But now they face a challenge that threatens the very survival of their business—rising health-care costs.

Most people will be drawn into the second story much more than the abstract comments of the first. Audiences develop relationships to the stories. Numbers are only numbers. Abstractions are only abstractions. They draw intellectual responses from the audience. But people elicit a human, emotive response. Audience members identify with Dino and Artie. They can see themselves in the struggles of these two businessmen. Dino's and Artie's story brings the issue down to earth and makes it real.

Whenever possible, incorporate stories into your speech. Bear in mind, however, that these stories need to be focused on making a point. A string of interesting anecdotes might be amusing, but it would hardly constitute a speech. A speech needs to make a point. But using stories can make a deeper point than facts alone.

Another way to use others' stories is to incorporate endorsements from people who benefit from making or using your product, service, or idea. This is especially true if you're a nonprofit organization. Nothing is more convincing than relating your story through the eyes of the people you serve. It's called *third-party endorsement*.

SPEAK ABOUT WHAT YOU KNOW

The best way to put yourself into a speech is to speak about what you know. Don't accept a speaking engagement on which you cannot deliver. When asked why he never painted angels, renowned artist Gustave Courbet replied "because I have never seen one."

Executives are called on to speak on a wide range of topics, from the economic outlook to the value of Little League baseball. Worthwhile topics, to be sure, but there's nothing worse than sitting through a presentation that lacks conviction, firsthand observation, and emotion. It has been suggested that we persuade with reason but motivate with emotion. Emotion, conviction, and firsthand observations are invariably missing when presenters speak on topics they know little about and to which they have little or no commitment.

It's easy to spot such a speech. The presenter seems bored. The material lacks imagination and is void of firsthand accounts and reactions. It's presented without any feeling. Invariably, this kind of talk is read more than spoken. Invariably, it fails.

It's therefore essential for you to talk about what you know, a subject about which you have strong viewpoints. It's better to turn down a speaking engagement than address a topic with which you have limited knowledge and little feeling. Simply suggest to those who invited you to speak that there are other topics you feel more comfortable talking about and find out if they're amenable to adjusting their agenda.

If they won't accept your suggested topic, offer to help locate a more appropriate presenter. People who put programs together deserve your courtesy and your help. In addition, they can be enormously valuable resources. You want their goodwill. At some future time, they could provide you with a platform that enables you to reach a key audience with a meaningful message. So suggest an alternative speaker. But decline to speak on an assigned topic yourself if you're not a cheerleading expert in the field.

Chapter Checklist

Put Yourself into the Speech

- Are there any points in the speech where you can insert an appropriate personal anecdote?
- Are there any places where you need a good story about someone else? Can you find a story through library research, friends, or your own recollections?
- Do you have too many *I* stories? Do they all serve to make a point? If not, eliminate the superfluous ones.
- Before accepting a speaking engagement, is the topic something you know well and are comfortable discussing? If not, is your host willing to modify the topic, or can you suggest a more appropriate speaker?

Death by Oratory

A megalomaniac droned on and on about his own life. The stories were entertaining to him, but only to him. Everyone else was bored and frustrated. The only common theme was that every story related to his life. The audience knew his opinions on everything, but didn't take much else away from the speech. It was a clear case of involvement taken to extremes.

- Don't talk about yourself unless it serves a clear purpose in making a point in your speech.
- Don't talk about others in negative terms. They are not there to defend themselves, so don't be a bully.
- Don't use the term *my*, which implies possession and self-centeredness. Instead, use *I* statements to discuss how you feel, what you have seen, and where you have been, and *we* statements to draw your audience in.
- Don't offer opinions about subjects in which you have no expertise. Probably, no one really cares.
- Don't strip your speech of anything personal or it could be delivered by anyone. And the audience might wonder why you are delivering it.

Chapter Eight

Use Humor and Numbers

H umor and numbers are the spice of speeches: Too little and the speech may feel bland or lifeless; too much and they can burn the mouth. The trick is to get just the right kinds of humor and numbers in the right amounts. These and other details may seem small, but they are a vital part of crafting an effective speech.

USE HUMOR WISELY

A funny thing may happen on the way to your speech . . . You may find that a great joke—the one that sent you beating the floor with your fists when you heard it—has lost its punch. The audience is not rolling in the aisles. They are only snickering politely. The joke is on you. Should you use humor in your presentation? The answer is yes and no.

Humor can be fun. It can be entertaining. People respond favorably to other people who make them laugh. That accounts for the popularity of comedy clubs and the universal love for good comedians. There's even a 24-hour comedy television channel. Humor can make us feel good. But, it can also be explosive. As such, it should be treated with care.

Humor is tricky—even for the best comedians. Consider that professional comedians such as Johnny Carson and Jay Leno have paid writers cranking out bits for them. They select the best of these and weave them together in an opening monologue. They rehearse the jokes and then deliver them, drawing on years of experience in making audiences laugh. Even with all these resources, talent, and preparation, observe how many of the jokes of professional comics don't elicit a laugh from the audience.

Professional humorists are skilled at recovering from jokes that don't work. They'll respond with some repartee about the quality of the writing staff, or, shaking their heads, "This is a tough audience here tonight."

As a speaker, you can't roll out a whole string of jokes and hope that one or two tickle people's fancy. You have room for one or two, if that. And you don't have years of experience in making audiences laugh. So your risks are much higher.

Humor can also backfire. What might be funny to you, the storyteller, could potentially be offensive to the listener.

There are several ways to take advantage of the power of humor while minimizing the risks:

USE HUMOR TO MAKE A POINT

Some speakers start their presentation with their favorite joke, even if it bears no relationship to the topic. This is based on the assumption that the audience needs to be primed or warmed up before you can turn to the serious (and perhaps boring) topic at hand. Unless you are a professional comedian, the audience is probably expecting to hear about your topic. The joke then becomes an unnecessary, perhaps risky, and even annoying diversion.

If, on the other hand, you can use humor to drive home a point, then it serves a purpose. It can be a way to warm up the audience while moving your speech forward. This is the best kind of humor. Even if the humor doesn't leave the listeners doubled over in their seats, it at least helps get them thinking about the topic.

Making a point also means that you don't leave the joke at the punchline waiting for the laughter (which may or may not materialize). You have already gone on to draw a moral from the story.

For example, you might start off a discussion of using cross-functional teams to solve company problems this way:

> I read recently about a veterinarian and a taxidermist who decided to share a shop in a small town in Ohio. The sign in the front window read: "Either way, you get your dog back."
> There is an important lesson there. We need to work together to solve our problems. People from marketing need to work with operations people. Designers need to work with engineers. Then, when we find a problem that one part of the organization can't solve, someone else may suggest a solution. It doesn't matter who comes up with the solution. The important thing is to "get the dog back."

USE HUMOROUS STORIES

A real story is less risky than a joke, just as nonfiction is less risky to write than fiction. Even if people are not impressed by a real story, at least it is real. But a fictitious story that falls flat is twice cursed, once because it failed, and second because someone took the trouble to make up this failure. Audiences are more forgiving about real life than they are about fantasy.

The best stories are personal, humorous ones. Sometimes even a story about an unrelated event can be tied in. An economist explaining an obtuse concept to a lay audience starts:

> I was told to present this material so even a four-year-old could understand it. Well, I tried it out on my four-year-old daughter. I have to admit, it's not quite there yet. Her response was, "That's nice, Daddy. Now can I have a lollipop?" I hope you'll be able to follow the presentation—but if I lose you anywhere, please ask. And if you need some incentive to stay with me, I still have a few lollipops left in my pocket.

Personal experiences or anecdotes are suitable grabbers. And if you don't have any great stories going into the room, keep your eyes open along the way or after you get there. Remember the green sneaker story I described in Chapter 2. Successful comics used to start their routines by recounting: "A funny thing happened to me on the way to the show tonight." If something funny did happen, try to work it in. It may be corny, but it is also effective. Most important: It's real. It's personal. It's you.

As noted in the previous chapter, anecdotes make you interesting because people like stories. They also carry conviction because you're talking about events you experienced firsthand.

MAKE YOURSELF THE BUTT OF THE JOKE

Obviously, if you are standing on the podium telling ethnic jokes, you're asking for trouble. But even jokes that appear to you to be innocuous can offend listeners. It is very hard to overestimate the sensitivity of audiences. Therefore, it's best to make yourself the butt of the joke. Making fun of yourself is least likely to offend anyone else. Personal stories, focusing on your own life or shortcomings, can often accomplish this.

USE QUOTES

As mentioned, quotes, proverbs, or sayings are also good grabbers, as well as good vehicles for using humor, because someone else actually does the talking.

Humorist Erma Bombeck suggests never using a doctor whose plants have died in the waiting room.

Should anyone take exception to the quote, you are not the offending party, the person quoted is. And if that someone is Mark Twain or Ben Franklin, chances are they—and you—will be forgiven.

USE CARTOONS

If you are using overheads or slides, cartoons or other humorous visuals can be a good way to grab attention and draw the audience into the talk. Showing a cartoon at the start of the presentation or in the middle can counter the soporific effect of watching visuals in a darkened room.

USE NUMBERS TO MAKE POINTS

Like humor, numbers can liven up a speech—or kill it. Statistics can be powerful convincers, punctuating a speech and anchoring it like stakes holding down a tent. Too few stakes and the tent blows away. Too many of them and the speech becomes impersonal and pinned down by these numbers.

Someone once suggested that if you "torture" numbers enough, they'll show what you want them to show. The trick is to torture your numbers until they sing, rather than torturing your audience. Here are some thoughts on how best to use them.

ROUND OFF

Comparative numbers are common, whether you're comparing last year's earnings versus this year's, or whether you're comparing the percentage of people unemployed from one month to the next. One way you can use such analyses to your advantage is to round them off. During the 1992 election campaign, for example, Ross Perot responded to critics who charged he was buying the election by pointing out that with six months left to go in the campaign, the Republicans and Democrats had each spent $17 million, but that he had spent "under $1.4 million." Perot might have spent $1.399 million. But under $1.4 million is even more dramatic.

Retailers understand this concept well. An item may be priced at $14.99, which seems to be considerably less than $15. So if you're trying to show value in a program or an item, use the "less than" technique instead of the actual number itself.

On the other hand, if you're trying to emphasize the largeness of the figure, then round up. "Our organization has more than 3 million members."

USE PROPORTIONS

Proportioning is another good technique to use when dealing with statistics, especially when you might have to increase prices. The increase at first might sound astronomical, until you point out that it will only increase the cost of a cigarette carton by 50 cents or "less than a penny a week." This breaking down of the increased cost by individual packages or units tends to minimize opposition.

This technique can also be used to provide a powerful demonstration of how small a number is, as in the case of a punishment for a crime.

I recently observed this technique on television. One of the three networks was doing a story about the lack of safety on our nation's highways. They attributed the problem to truck drivers who drive long distances and might not have time to properly maintain their vehicles, or might indulge in one drink too many in order to offset the monotony and loneliness of the road. The story was told through the eyes of one family who lost their son and five of his friends in an accident caused by a drunk truck driver—who was fined, then released.

A mother of one of the victims observed, "the total fine levied against the driver was $50, and that comes to less than $8.50 a life;" a powerful punctuation of numbers, making this a nearly unforgettable story. Using this technique adds enormous impact to any figures you use and dramatically brings them to life.

MAKE COMPARISONS

Although stretching dollar bills, automobiles, or other items end to end from the Earth to the Moon is an analogy that is somewhat overused, translating large numbers into more easily grasped subjects can be very effective in hammering home a point. One of my fellow speech trainers tells the story of an executive who, in his remarks, was bemoaning the fact that over the past 12 months, his industry had lost 350,000 workers. He skillfully used comparisons by adding "that equated to the entire work force of the state of Minnesota," thereby underscoring the enormity of the tragedy.

A nuclear power plant points out that annual radiation from the surrounding area is less than the solar radiation of a single cross-country airline flight and much less than a standard X-ray. This means a lot more than telling listeners how many millirems of radiation are released.

If the amount of zeros appears inordinately high, you can point out that "relative to what other organizations in your field are spending, the funds you're committing are low." Similarly, you can suggest this expenditure is consistent with what your organization has always appropriated to similar undertakings and consistent with what other area entities spend.

USE PERCENTAGES

Using percentages can help put numbers into perspective. A $200 million expenditure for research and development may sound extraordinarily high to some people, until you note that you have $20 billion in worldwide sales, bringing the R&D amount to only 1 percent of your total revenues.

Percentages can help large numbers look small. They can also make small numbers look large. If you had six customers last year and attracted six new ones this year, you could say your clientele has gone up 100 percent or doubled. This example also illustrates the need to balance presenting numbers favorably with the need to communicate openly and honestly. If the numbers become too good to be true, then you could erode your credibility with the audience.

QUANTIFY THE CONSEQUENCES

Numbers can be extremely effective in attaching a quantity to vague benefits or consequences. If you say that a company stands to lose a lot of money down the road if it doesn't follow your plan, that is much less effective than if you tell executives they could lose half a million dollars.

By quantifying the benefits, you may suggest that the money you're spending is an investment rather than an expense. If you can show that a $2.5 million appropriation of funds for a similar research project several years ago generated a new business with annual sales in excess of a quarter of a billion dollars (sounds more impressive than $250 million), the expenditure sounds like a good idea. It will pay for itself more than 100 times over.

By quantifying the consequences of taking an action or not taking an action, you may be able to show that it will be too costly to stand still. You might be able to point out that if the company doesn't pay $50,000 for a new roof now, it could end up paying more than $1 million for a new roof, new interior, and new equipment because of water damage. It doesn't take a mathematical genius to figure out that addition.

Effectively, powerfully, imaginatively, and properly used, statistics can be extraordinary motivators.

Chapter Checklist

Use Humor and Numbers

Use humor wisely

- Is the humor in your speech used to make a point?
- Does every piece of humor have a follow-up line emphasizing the point, which can be used if laughter doesn't follow?
- Could the humor be offensive to anyone in the audience?
- If you need to add humor, is there a funny story about yourself that fits with the topic?
- Can you find a good, humorous quote related to your topic?

Use numbers to make a point

- Do you have enough numbers in your speech to firmly anchor it?
- Examine each number in your speech. What point does it make? Can a different form or description of the number be more effective in making the point?
- Can you use rounding off, comparisons, and percentages to better make your points?
- Are there broad consequences discussed that can be quantified?

Death by Oratory

The most deadly sin in humor and numbers is gluttony. If you try to use every funny thing you ever heard, your speech will become so light it will float away. If you plug in every number you have heard, your speech will become so heavy it will sink like a stone. Moderation is the key.

- Don't put a number or a piece of humor in a speech unless it serves some purpose. There should be nothing extraneous to the theme of the speech, no matter how interesting it may be.
- If you have two numbers in a row, that's one too many. Find a way to cut one unless it is absolutely necessary. If the speech starts looking like the U.S. federal budget, take out all the numbers and start again.
- If a humorous anecdote goes on for more than two minutes, see if you can condense it. Your audience will be a lot more forgiving if you try something short. A long lead-in raises expectations, while brevity is the essence of good communications.
- Putting in numbers or humor to kill time will also kill the speech.

TECHNIQUE

Now you know *what* constitutes a great speech—a solid structure and exciting texture. Next, we can get down to the nuts and bolts of work.

How do you deal with the thousands of details that go into taking you from a speaking engagement to a polished performance? How do you find out about your audience? How long should you write? When should you start? How can you use visuals most effectively? Should you work with a speechwriter? How do you introduce another speaker?

Chapter Nine

Know Your Audience and Setting

A n oil executive once spoke to a group about challenges in the industry. He frequently referred to the processing of "tars and oils." When he received a transcript of his remarks to review, he found that, according to the transcriber, he had actually discussed "Tarzan oils." Most of his audience probably knew what he was saying, but the transcriber obviously had no idea. He was discussing a black, gooey substance, while at least one listener was imagining glistening biceps swinging through the jungles. The latter may have actually been a more interesting speech, but it was not the one he intended to deliver.

It is vital to know where your audience is coming from—their understanding of the subject matter, background, interests and reasons for being there. Clearly, you would not deliver the same message to a high school graduating class that you would to your board of directors or your stockholders.

You should get a sense of what the audience's expectations are for the encounter. If it is a speech at the end of an all-day event that they are required to attend, they may be less receptive than if it is at the beginning of an event they requested to attend.

When you are invited to speak, your audience probably has expectations about what it will receive from you. If you are Jay Leno, they probably expect to have a few laughs. If you are the leading expert on environmental consulting, they would expect you to discourse boldly on the Earth Summit or the ozone layer. If, instead, you launched into a diatribe against the antisocial lyrics of popular music, you might lose a few people.

These expectations need to be balanced against your own

agenda. Your audience may want to be entertained, but you may want to sell them a specific message. Try to compromise. Give an entertaining speech that manages to deliver the message you want to convey. Don't offend them. But say what you have to say.

Work within the constraints of your audience's expectations. Mark Antony said he came not to praise Caesar but to bury him. So he lied. But that was the message his audience wanted to hear. If he had said he came to praise Caesar, the crowd wouldn't have given him five minutes. Appreciate where your audience is coming from and meet them halfway.

The speech can be like a candlelit dinner. You are the host. You have to keep your guests entertained. And you have to keep them engaged. Otherwise, you are in it by yourself. A speech is a dance between what the audience knows and cares about and what you want to communicate.

Seize the opportunities at hand. Look for the possibilities of the event. Remember, President Lincoln's Gettysburg remarks were made during the dedication of a cemetery. Martin Luther King spoke during a march on Washington. Many others have spoken during such occasions and not left the world with any lasting result. There are no small events. Just small speeches.

SETTING

Another important piece of research is to find out the setting for the event. Maybe you can tell from the advance information that you will be speaking to a large crowd or a small, intimate gathering. But don't trust your assumptions. At a workshop of about 20 people recently, two of the senior executives on the program began their remarks by apologizing for having full, printed speeches without any visual aids. They had assumed the gathering would be larger and more formal.

Finding out the number of people expected to attend can be a useful first start for gauging the setting of the event. A smaller group will tend to be somewhat less formal and lend itself to the use of overheads. If it is extremely informal, you will probably want to scrap your prepared text in favor of notecards.

But size doesn't always tell you what's going on. A small group could be sitting in a classroom arrangement with a lectern at the front of the room. Or it could be arranged around a single table or a group of circular tables.

While you are researching the setting, also find out about the location in which you are going to make the presentation. Is it a small room? How will tables be arranged? Is there a raised stage? A lectern? Is there a "green room" for speakers backstage or should you sit in the front of the audience?

You can also check at this time to make sure that you will have access to any audiovisual resources you need. Does the room have a built-in projection system? Does it have a screen for slides and overheads? Can you get into the room in advance to run through your materials and test the equipment?

Finally, you may be able to find out about the history of the building in which you will be speaking. If the location has a specific significance, don't overlook that as a possible element in your speech. Some historic buildings have brochures written about them. If it seems like the location for your speech might have some special meaning, you might ask organizers if they have information about the building, campus, or city in which you will be speaking. Even if you can't get it directly from the source, you might want to track down this information in your research.

For example, if you were speaking about the future of computers at the University of Pennsylvania, you might want to refer to the fact that the first computer was invented there. If you were speaking in St. Louis, you might make reference to its role as a gateway to settlers headed to the West. If these references are not too forced, they can enhance the speech and give it a personal and specific flavor that ties it directly to the location of the event taking place.

DO YOUR HOMEWORK

How do you find out about the audience and setting for your speech? In a word: Ask. I find myself calling my host two or three times in advance of a speech in order to ascertain who will be coming to hear me. I even ask for a list of attendees. I just want to make certain I'm presenting what the audience expects to hear.

Assessing an audience's level of understanding might also necessitate your modifying or adapting a specific speech to make it more understandable to a specific group.

So don't be shy about asking those who invite you to speak about the makeup of the audience. It's a sign that you care about your listeners. And, even if you ask some questions that may appear to be ignorant, better to embarrass yourself in front of one organizer than a roomful of people. It's essential you know whom you're addressing before you begin speaking.

QUESTIONS TO ASK

Among the questions you might want to ask are:

- What is the size of the audience?
- What is the demographic, ethnic, and gender mix of the audience?
- What are the career positions of audience members? (Are they plant workers, middle managers, or CEOs?)
- Why are they there?
- What knowledge and experience do they have with your subject? Are they very sophisticated or do they expect a presentation geared for a lay audience?
- Are they likely to be receptive or skeptical, even hostile?
- If they are a group that comes together regularly, have they ever had a presentation on your subject in the past? If so, can you obtain a summary or copy of it? Who gave it? How was it received?
- Are there any guests or participants who should be acknowledged?
- What is the room setup? Will there be a lectern and microphone? Will there be audiovisual equipment for presentations?

- Can the organizers send you a brochure or other background on the group and the meeting place? Is there any special history of the building or city in which the event is taking place that you should know about?
- What is the purpose of the meeting?
- Who are the other speakers on the program? What are their topics? Can you receive advance copies of their remarks?
- Who will be introducing you? (You might want to make a point of thanking that person.)
- Who will open the Q&A (you or your host)?
- Is the Q&A immediately after your remarks? How long should it last?
- Who will close your part of the program?
- Will you need to introduce the next speaker? (If so, you will need some background information.)

Hosts are usually very helpful in providing such information to speakers. You are their guest and they usually want to help you do the best job possible with your speech. But occasionally, you will reach a contact that either doesn't know what the event is going to look like or doesn't want to spend the time talking about it. Get what you can from your first contact and then ask if there is someone involved in the event who has a better knowledge of the audience.

If you are dealing with someone who has not organized many events, you may also need to help walk them through the things they need to think about before the event. They may not have a sense of the many issues that need to be dealt with. They will be forced to decide them eventually, but that will be too late to help you. So, walk them through your questions if you have to, but make sure you get an answer—even if you have to make it up yourself. Don't leave these issues to chance.

Finally, don't be shy about suggesting on your own:

- Topics.
- Formats.

- Room layouts.
- Amenities.

Sometimes, these suggestions can improve both the speech and the overall event.

Chapter Checklist

Know Your Audience and Setting

- Do you understand what the audience expects of you?
- Why would they be interested in your subject?
- Have you called ahead to talk to the organizers of the event about the audience and expectations for the speech? Have you called back later with any questions that were not completely answered?
- Can you describe with confidence the audience and setting for your speech? If not, you need to ask more questions.
- Have you asked as many of the questions at the end of the chapter as are relevant to the situation?
- Have you made any suggestions on the setting that will make your presentation more appealing?

Death by Oratory

An apocryphal story tells how a speaker once was going to address the handicapped bowler's league. He never called his host to check on the audience because he assumed that the name said it all. He carefully prepared his remarks to focus on issues related to disabled athletes. He was prepared to commend them on their tenacity and courage in pursuing athletic activities in the face of physical disabilities. As he stood at the lectern and looked across the audience, he suddenly noticed that there was not a wheelchair in the house. *Handicap* referred to their bowling scores. The only thing disabled was his speech.

This underscores the following principles:

- Don't assume anything. If there is the least trace of doubt in your mind, ask.

- Don't stop searching until you find someone who has direct knowledge of the audience (or is a part of it). There are plenty of well-meaning people who can lead you astray.

- Question anything about the information you are receiving that sounds suspicious. (Is it likely that a town of your size would have enough members for its own handicapped bowler's association? Have you ever heard of one before?)

- Don't forget to do your homework. A quick investigation of bowling, which would be a useful prelude to writing the speech, would probably have turned up the term *handicap* in reference to the sport. That could have raised a question that would have saved a lot of heartache.

Chapter Ten

Make Visuals Work for You

G ood slides, overheads, flip charts, and videotapes can enhance any presentation, making it attractive and interesting
while reinforcing the ideas you are communicating. Bad visuals
can leave your audience squinting, overloaded with information,
lost, confused, frightened, frustrated, or angry. Bad use of visuals
can leave the audience feeling abandoned while you are off playing with what may appear to be beautiful pictures.

CHOOSE YOUR WEAPON: FLIP CHARTS, OVERHEADS, SLIDES

Flip charts work well in small groups. They are easy to handle
and easy to follow. The same holds true for overheads. Both are
especially well suited to the more energetic professorial presenters who like to move around a lot rather than remain anchored
at the lectern.

Overheads also work well with larger groups, providing you
have the assistance of someone to change them at the appropriate
moment. It's important to work out some kind of signal in advance to let the person assisting you know it's time to change the
transparency. Nothing is more tedious, more distracting, than a
speaker repeatedly saying, "May we please see the next transparency or slide?" A rehearsal is also a good idea, possibly elim-
inating the need for signals. The assistant may then be able to
follow your presentation, and armed with a set of written cues,
know exactly when to change the overheads.

Slides work best for larger audiences. Although some presenters use overheads (rather than slides) for audiences as large as 300, my own rule of thumb is:

- Flip charts for 20 people and under.
- Overheads for 21 to 50 people.
- Slides for more than 50 people.

I resist using slides, especially in small groups, because they usually require darkening a room and I hate losing eye contact with my audience. But I recognize that in a large, crowded room they are often the visual of choice.

I once attended a quality seminar with Dr. W. Edwards Deming, in which he used technology to overcome the constraints of a large conference room. Two wide-screen televisions in the middle of the audience allowed them to see close up what was taking place on stage. The monitors also showed the overheads, so the more than 100 people from front to back had a fairly good view of the presentation without having to dim the lights for slides.

KEEP THEM CLEAR

Be careful in choosing your method of visual communication—improper use of slides or overheads can ruin rather than enhance a presentation.

For example, avoid putting too many words on your visuals, whether you're using slides or transparencies. This can intimidate and confuse an audience by overwhelming them with too much visual material. Also, more words require smaller lettering, making it especially difficult for the audience to read. The more focused listeners become on reading your visuals, the less attention they will give to your speech.

Less is more. Use single words or short phrases that summarize the material you plan to cover. Also, use other illustrations and graphics. As mentioned earlier, cartoons can help inject humor into the speech.

Remember that participants come to see and hear you. Visuals are merely the scenery, or at best, supporting actors. Many presenters make the mistake of trying to have the visuals tell the whole story. They should instead be used as marquees to attract the audience's attention and pique peoples' interest in the subject. They are simply headlines inviting the listener to know more.

KEEP THE VISUALS DYNAMIC

Equally important, remember that you lead the visuals. Too many presenters flash a slide or transparency, then turn away from the audience and read it verbatim. This is poor presentation technique. It's tedious. It puts your worst side to the audience (assuming, of course, that they would rather look at your face!). It slows down a presentation and it's insulting to the audience, most of whom (it is assumed) can read for themselves.

You should be so familiar with your material that you rarely, if ever, have to reassure yourself that the right visual is up. The preferred technique is to look at the audience while the new visual comes up, and with good eye contact, paraphrase or elaborate on the "bullet points" that appear.

The visual should be like the assistant in a magic show—adding life to the presentation but not distracting attention from the show at hand. Visuals can create a smoother and more interesting presentation, but they need to be kept in their place.

USE VISUALS TO REINFORCE YOUR ROAD MAP

If you have between three and six (or more) topics to cover, visuals can be very useful in helping to reinforce your road map. You can list all the points to be covered in your speech and then refer back to them during the speech. You have now preconditioned the audience to receive, process, and react to your information, making them likely to be more attentive, more receptive.

One very effective way to signal your progress through the speech with visuals is through "build slides." The first slide might have one bullet point, and then more are added as you reach each key concept in your speech. For example, a speech about the company's history, present challenges, and future prospects could use the following three overheads:

Overhead 1   Our Company
                • A History of Innovation

Overhead 2   Our Company
                • A History of Innovation
                • Present Challenges

Overhead 3   Our Company
                • A History of Innovation
                • Present Challenges
                • Our Shining Future

Upon reaching the next point to be covered by the talk, the speaker puts up the next "build slide." Listeners can then see clearly where they have been and where they are. The current topic can also be highlighted on the slide or overhead. Another option is to have the entire road map on every slide, but only reveal one bullet point at a time.

MOTION TO EVOKE EMOTION

Videotape and film are also effective presentation enhancers. I find a VCR with a remote control switch especially helpful. That way I don't have to move back and forth between "home base" and the video equipment. If you have more than one video to show, put them on one reel with a five-second stop between each segment. That way, after finishing the first segment, you can speak to the audience before going to the next one, and you never have to go back to the tape deck to cue another tape.

For a large audience, you might consider using a video projector (such as Sharp's "Sharpvision" LCD Video Projector). It projects your video onto a large screen, making it appear enormous.

A less expensive alternative is to have two or three video monitors strategically located throughout the room.

New computer-based presentation technologies are appearing on the scene every day. I recently observed a very impressive presentation by the CFO of a foreign company at a large Wall Street investment banking firm. The speaker, by himself, might have been a bit boring. With a heavy accent, he had to carefully enunciate every syllable to be understood. But the visuals from the electronic laserdisc system were so powerful and exciting that the audience stayed with him every step of the way.

Computer-based presentation systems allow the presenter to combine computer animation, video, and slides into a single presentation. Another system I witnessed recently used a laptop computer and a Sony CRV laserdisc player to project images onto a screen or a large-screen television monitor. The system, operated by a technician, allowed the speaker to use special effects such as "page-turns," "flips," and "wipes."

There are new technologies appearing constantly, as computers become smaller and both hardware and software become more advanced. Kodak's new Photo CD player, for example, will allow anyone to put up to 100 photos on a compact disc as easily as developing a roll of film, for a price that is comparable to buying a music CD. Additional equipment will allow users with a little computer skill to edit images and add music or other enhancements.

TECHNOLOGY'S ACHILLES' HEEL

This new technology may have eliminated some of the pitfalls of technology past. Gone are the days of presenters being embarrassed by upside-down slides or slides that "melt" in the projector. But the bigger the technological leaps, the farther you have to fall.

The more your presentation is dependent on technology, the more important it is to get to the location in advance, set up, and check out the equipment. It is also important to have someone along to operate the system. Because this requires teamwork, it is vital that you run through the presentation with the audiovisuals several times to work out the bugs. You also need someone either physically present or available by phone, who knows how to fix the system.

No matter how well you prepare, you can still get caught by a system that crashes in the middle of your presentation. Don't let it make your presentation crash as well. As is the rule in all computer systems, there should be enough redundancy and backups to handle unexpected contingencies. Be sure you have spare copies of disks containing the program, extra batteries for laptops, extra dubs of videotapes, and even extra bulbs for your overhead or slide projectors.

Finally, you should be prepared to deliver your speech even if technology fails you. You should never be so dependent on the equipment that your entire speech falls apart if the power goes out. The speech may lose some of its flair and excitement without your audiovisuals, but they should be an enhancement to the presentation, not the entire presentation. If the speech can't stand on its own, you are very vulnerable to technology failure.

PEOPLE DON'T COME TO SEE MACHINES

Even worse than the threat of a hardware or software crash, if your speech cannot stand alone without the technology, it means you have yielded too much power of the speech to the machines. People don't come to hear and see machines—even very clever ones. They come to hear and see speakers.

The key to successful audiovisuals is to keep them in their place. If you make the audience focus too much on them, you lose their attention. The audience is there to hear you. Too much focus on a video, for example, could make the audience forget about you and perhaps resist your ideas when you do appear.

Shimmering technology can be so seductive that it ends up

taking over your speech. To test whether you are too dependent on the technology, imagine making the presentation without the audiovisual aids. If the speech dies, you need to pay more attention to your words and throttle back on the fireworks.

GOOD THEATER

Good videotape or film can serve as a powerful grabber. You're introduced. But you don't appear. The house lights dim. The music hits. The video comes up. This can be an enormously effective opening.

Theatricality! Staging! Pace! These all play a role in a successful presentation. Starting with a powerful video—especially after you've been introduced but not yet appeared—adds the aura of mystery and surprise. These, in turn, add theatricality, staging, and pace.

In sum, good visuals, skillfully orchestrated and smoothly interwoven into a speech, will clearly enhance that presentation and likely get an audience to react favorably toward you and your message.

Chapter Checklist

Make Visuals Work for You

- Have you incorporated visuals in your speech? Will they be clear to everyone in the room?
- Do all your visuals serve an important purpose in carrying forward your speech?
- Are your visuals entertaining?
- Do you have the right visuals for the size and setting of the presentation?

Death by Oratory

A senior manager making a presentation to a small group begins by tossing a transparency onto the overhead projector. She then hovers over the transparency like a chef tending a steak on the grill. Except there's just one problem. No sizzle. The overhead is tough—very tough. The type is microscopic and there are lines all over the place. It is as if this manager tried to cram her Ph.D. thesis onto this one little sheet. The smart members of the audience know they're not being served prime cuts, and politely decline. The audience breathes a sigh of relief when the transparency is lifted from the projector. But wait . . . she has another one! The only silver lining is that the manager is so caught up in her overheads that she doesn't have to watch the audience slipping away.

- Don't use overheads for large audiences, or slides for small, intimate audiences. Match the visuals to the setting.
- Don't use complicated visuals. If you can't make it simple, throw it out.
- Don't turn your back to the audience to read your visuals. Most audiences are capable of reading, and they want to see your smiling face.

Chapter Eleven

Sweat the Details
Length, Formatting, and Resources

Y ou may have a good idea of what you want the speech to do, but it is how you carry out this vision that will determine if you create a great speech. There are many small details that confront you when you sit down to write your first draft. In this section, we address some of these details:

- How much time to allow for planning the speech.
- How long to make the first draft.
- When to use full text and when to use notecards.
- How to get pronunciation right.
- How to build a resource library and folder.

HOW FAR IN ADVANCE SHOULD YOU START?

If you book the speaking engagement a year in advance, start then. In other words, you can never start preparing too soon. If you have several speeches to deliver in the next year, keep them on a list in your calendar or in an "upcoming speech" folder. Put them at the bottom on your "to do" list. Then you can scan the horizon for great newspaper and magazine articles related to the subject, quotes that work, and, in particular, a strong grabber. You can also be gathering notes on your own personal stories or internal memos that can contribute to your presentation. The worst thing is to sit down to write your speech and not have enough materials.

This pre-preparation stage takes little or no time, just attention. It merely requires keeping your eyes open as you go about your life. Look at everything that comes into your line of sight (or hearing) as a potential contribution to the speech.

While this pre-preparation should start immediately, the intensive period of writing and rehearsal should begin at least three weeks before the speech date. This allows roughly one week for writing, one week for revisions, and one week for rehearsals. If you need to develop overheads or slides, these steps may have to be completed earlier.

The speech-preparation process requires blocks of uninterrupted time. While writing, you don't want every great thought to be interrupted by phone calls or visitors. While rehearsing, you won't be able to work on your timing and pacing unless you can run through the entire speech. You might want to start writing the speech at night or on the weekend. Or you can shut the door and defer phone calls while writing during the workday. However you do it, you will need uninterrupted time to write, revise, and rehearse the speech.

Block off a total of about five to 10 hours, preferably in one- or two-hour blocks, to work on the first draft. Plan to spend two to five hours revising the speech. Then plan on at least two or three rehearsals (20 to 30 minutes each for a 20-minute speech). Write these on your calendar so you can be sure you have enough time. Keep track of how much time it actually takes you to prepare your speech. Maybe you can create the speech in less time than suggested here, or maybe you need to allow for more time. If the speech is very important, you will want to spend extra time getting it just right.

HOW MANY PAGES TO WRITE?

How long is a 20-minute speech? Twenty minutes, obviously. How many pages or words it takes to cross these 20 minutes depends somewhat on your speaking style. You will have to time the speech as you practice it and tune it up or down to meet your specific requirements. As a general rule for the first draft, a 20-minute speech runs about 2,000 words or about eight double-spaced pages. This is based on an average speaking rate of 100 words per minute.

As you become more sophisticated in giving speeches, you might want to come up with your own average speaking rate. With modern word processing software, it is usually quite easy to get a word count on your speech. Once you have the count, time how long it takes you to deliver the speech. Then use the following formula:

$$\frac{\text{Number of words}}{\text{Time to deliver (minutes)}} = \text{Speaking rate (words per minute)}$$

Write this number down and stick it in your speech background folder, or put it in your Rolodex under "Speeches." The next time you need to draft a speech, you only need to multiply the number of minutes in the speech by your speaking rate. You will then have a very good estimate of how many words you need for your first draft. This can save you a lot of time editing a speech that is running too long, or fortifying a speech that is too short.

KEEP IT BRIEF

William Shakespeare said "brevity is the soul of wit." Enough said.

Keep it short. Keep it simple. Sometimes you are told to deliver a 20-minute speech. If so, you have no choice but to deliver it for 20 minutes. But if you have a choice how long to go, don't spend a minute more than you need to. If you are scheduled for 20 minutes and then another 20 of questions and answers, don't drag on for 30 or 40, cutting the Q&A short. Your audience may be supportive in the beginning, but their eyes will start to glaze over just after you cross the 20-minute mark. By the end, they will be looking at their watches.

Be true to your agreement with the audience. If they've agreed to give you a certain amount of their time, your part of the contract is keep to schedule. This should not force you to sacrifice the content of your speech. You should be able to condense and sharpen your work to keep it short. You may even find it is more powerful for the effort. You may have to cut back on detail or even eliminate one or two of the points you had intended to make. This will force you to decide which are the key points to communicate, further strengthening the impact of the speech.

Once you've finished your first draft of the speech, go through it with a view toward editing. Look at every page, every sentence, every word and ask yourself: Is this necessary? Does it move the speech forward? If not, cut! Be ruthless. Be brutal. Don't listen if they beg for mercy. Let them go.

Many writers become attached to the things they write. They derive a narcissistic pleasure in hearing their own words. But the pleasure rapidly turns to torment when they stand writhing in front of an audience—their brilliant phrases falling flat. Don't be so attached to the beauty of your words that you cling to them when they are obviously not needed. Trust your intuition. When you feel excited about reading a section of the speech, hold onto it. But those parts of the speech you tend to skip over on each readthrough should be prime candidates for the shredder.

FORMAT: TEXT VERSUS CARDS

Unless you memorize your speech, formatting is an important consideration. Some speakers prefer to work from full text and others use only a set of note cards. Which format should you use, and how should you prepare it?

There is no standing rule for whether to use text or cards. It depends on the occasion, your familiarity with the material, and your own personal style. You will probably have to experiment a bit to find the approach that works best for you.

If you are very familiar with the material you are presenting, or if you have made a similar speech several times before, note cards will probably work very well. If this speech is new ground, then you will probably want to begin working with the full text, at least for rehearsals. As you work with the text, it may become more natural and flowing, in which case you may need nothing more than a few cards to get you rolling. Best of all, you might become so comfortable with your material that you'll require neither.

The greatest benefit of note cards is they allow you more eye contact with the audience. When this contact is particularly important—in a small group, for example—you should prepare to deliver the remarks with note cards. This allows you to speak directly to your audience. With a full text, you can maintain eye contact, as we will discuss later, by looking up at the end of each sentence. This will not, however, be as easily sustained as with cards.

One drawback to note cards, however, is that some speakers have a tendency to ramble. If you haven't learned the speech word for word, you will probably lose some of the ear appeal that you may have written into the original speech. You could be tempted to take detours and these can be disastrous. You might slip into patterns of *wells* or *uhs* as you try to find the right phrases. Note cards, therefore, should be used with caution. As for the uhs, rehearsals should help eliminate them.

The occasion will also suggest what type of format is most appropriate. If it is an informal farewell to a departing employee, you might be better off if you work from cards or, better yet, from memory. Here, polish is not as important as sincerity. If you are delivering a speech to hundreds of listeners, they expect the remarks to run smoothly and finish on time. Here, you would definitely want to have prepared text, unless you have memorized the remarks.

MAKING IT YOUR OWN

No matter what format you use for delivering the speech, it should probably start out as a full text. The full text is where you can work over the innuendos and the wording. It is where you can make sure that you are saying what you want to say. It is where you can determine pauses and other details of effective delivery.

As you work over your speech during rehearsals, you will probably make annotations on the text. Some speakers prefer a highlighter to emphasize key phrases. Others use pen to circle or underline key sections of the speech. In this way, the speaker can go right to the phrases that will trigger the train of thought. Then, as you stand at the lectern, you have your own personal road map to help you move quickly through the speech and ensure that you don't lose your place.

If you feel comfortable at this point, you might go to the next step of creating note cards with just those key highlighted words on them. Then you can practice delivering the speech from cards. You may even decide to dispose of the cards and give the speech from memory.

Memorizing a speech that you will only deliver once is very time-consuming and may not be worth the effort. Audiences, while they are impressed with a speaker who can deliver a substantial speech from memory, certainly do not expect it. Unless you can do it very smoothly and well, it is better to have some text or notes with you.

Even if you have memorized the speech, you might feel more secure having a few notes jotted down on cards. Taking these cards with you to the podium can give you the security of knowing that if your mind suddenly freezes and goes blank, you can refer to the cards and get back on track. The cards should follow the frame that you are using for the speech.

Your cards or text should include your grabber at the top or on the front page. But this should be memorized so you can deliver it looking right at the audience. It is useful to keep it at the top of your speech as a reminder or if you need to refresh your memory before going on. You might want to draw a large arrow at the point where your memorized text ends and you return to your written text so you don't have to search for the spot. You should try to memorize your conclusion as well.

LAYOUT

You need to print the speech in a large, dark typeface such as Presentations that you can read while standing upright at the lectern. A small typeface could cause you to lose your place or force you to bend over the lectern, which would detract from the power of your delivery. Use upper- and lowercase, rather than all caps, because it makes it easier to scan.

Most speakers like the speech to be double- or triple-spaced and pages to be numbered, just in case the entire speech tumbles onto the floor as they are walking up to the stage. (If you are using note cards, it is especially important to number them, because they are much harder to hold on to.)

You might want to forestall this unlikely calamity by putting the speech into a folder or even a pocket folder. One particularly elegant solution is a portfolio produced by Script-Master, which contains the speech before its delivery, displays two entire pages of the speech at once, and facilitates sliding pages smoothly.

Other speakers (particularly men, who have the advantage of large pockets in their suit jackets) keep the text in their breast pocket, taking it out when they reach the podium. The drawback to this approach is the speech has a permanent crease in the center of it, which may make it harder to slide the pages. It also means there will be a point at the beginning of the speech when the speaker unfolds and straightens the pages. Unless you have a tendency to misplace small folders (an affliction that besets many of us), it is probably better to use a folder.

Don't staple the speech. If you don't have a secure folder, use a paper clip or binding to hold the speech together. As you finish each page slide it across into the "out" pile. This avoids noisy flipping and page turning that can look like a fresh catch of herring doing somersaults on the deck of a fishing boat. This sideshow could distract listeners from the speech.

PRONUNCIATION

While you are working on the speech, be sure to check any unusual spellings or pronunciations. The personal references that are intended to endear you to the audience may have the opposite effect if you mispronounce someone's name. Even if it is a name you shouldn't be expected to know, mispronunciation may be read as a lack of interest or familiarity with the person you are mentioning.

Speechwriter Robert Reilly recalls writing a speech for a prominent television personality to deliver to a meeting of Catholic bishops. The speaker was known for his humor, so the speech was filled with one-liners. But the biggest laugh came when he unintentionally misread Vatican II (Vatican Two) as Vatican Eleven.[12]

Check out any terms and names you are not familiar with. Call the organizers. Or even contact the person you are mentioning, if you have to. Remember, it is better to be embarrassed in front of an audience of one than an audience of hundreds. Most people will be flattered that you took the time. And if their name is frequently mispronounced, they will be especially grateful. You may not even have to speak to the person directly. You can usually get a pronunciation from a secretary or even from a voice mail or message system on which the subject has pronounced his or her name.

As you read through the speech, be sure to write phonetic pronunciations after each name or word that may be difficult to pronounce. Look up pronunciations in the dictionary if they are words you do not commonly use. Even if they are words you know quite well from reading, that doesn't guarantee that you can pronounce them correctly. Take the extra time. Don't leave it to chance or trust your memory.

WHAT RESOURCES DO YOU NEED?

The best resources are a command of the subject, a lively wit, and a practiced skill with words, preparation, and rehearsal. Of course, we can't all write like Shakespeare, and I am sure Shakespeare even had his moments. At these times—when you are searching for just the right word, or the right quote—it can be handy to have several additional resources at your side as you craft your speech. Most of these are the "usual suspects," but it is important to pay attention to how you use them.

A good thesaurus is a must. You may have a phrase that makes perfect sense but falls flat to the ear. A thesaurus can suggest a word change that could make the phrase sing. A rhyming dictionary can also do the trick, provided you do not overuse it. You don't want the speech to sound like a nursery rhyme.

A good book of quotations is useful, especially if you have a quote but can't remember who said it. One important use for a book of quotations is to surround yourself with great thoughts. Here's how it works. You want to speak about leadership, but you are having trouble getting started. With a book of quotations you can gain a variety of different perspectives on the subject by looking under all the entries for leadership. You can hear John F. Kennedy remark, "It is time for a new generation of leadership, to cope with new problems and new opportunities." Then hear Havelock Ellis comment, "To be a leader of men one must turn one's back on men." Or Walter Lippmann: "The final test of a leader is that he leaves behind him in other men the conviction and the will to carry on." These perspectives can get you thinking. They can get your juices flowing. By looking at each one and discarding it, you may find yourself with a clearer view of your own thoughts on the subject. Without using any of these ideas directly, you have forged ideas of your own. Where else can you find such a distinguished group of orators and writers with whom to converse about a subject when you are working on a speech in the middle of the night?

HOMEMADE REFERENCES

The best reference materials are those that you construct out of your own experience. Keep a speech file. Fill it with the stories, quotes, and information that you come across in your daily life from newspapers, magazines, radio, or television. If something makes you smile or laugh, jot it down or tear it out of the newspaper. Keep a file for speech ideas and shove everything interesting in the file. If something strikes you as interesting, even if it seems like you could never in a million years find a way to relate it to a speech, hold onto it. Then someday, you will suddenly see a connection between a humorous story about Christopher Columbus and your speech on high technology.

To keep it simple, you should start out with a single speech file and stuff everything into it. When you sit down to write a speech, go through the file. It will be like looking at a personal scrapbook. You will experience the warmth of the old memories. You might find something that fits perfectly with the speech at hand. At the very least, it is a good way to start the thought process. You may be inspired to write something that moves your audience the way the statements and stories in your file move you.

If you speak regularly on certain subjects, it will be easier for you to collect information on specific topics in separate files. One executive keeps files on topics such as globalization, leadership, technology, and corporate governance. Then, when a speech comes up on a given topic, he has plenty of material. It also gives him a place to file those great articles that he comes across in magazines and newspapers. Before he started the filing system, he used to discard these articles with the magazine. Now he has a place where they can be filed and easily retrieved.

Consider creating your own subject files for topics on which you might be asked to speak. Then you can avoid costly library searches or time-consuming rummaging through back issues of *Fortune*. Once you have the system in place, it takes almost no time to tear out or copy articles to fill your files.

FACTS, FACTS, FACTS

If your own speech file is a bit on the light side, you may need to go searching for additional facts. If you have access to on-line databases (such as Lexis-Nexis), this search can be quite simple. If not, you still may be able to find the information you need without spending too many hours crawling through the stacks of the library.

If you don't have access to internal corporate researchers, then get to know your local reference librarian. If you have a less-than-complete library in your neighborhood, get to know the librarian in the next town. They probably won't ask where you are from, and are usually extremely helpful to anyone who walks into the door or calls on the phone. Reference librarians in the New York Public Library system answer more than 5 million questions every year,[13] so don't think that you are bothering them.

When you complete your first draft, look for places where it could benefit from an anecdote or factual information. Anecdotes can be found by looking through guides to current magazine and newspaper articles on your topic (such as the *Reader's Guide to Periodical Literature*). Facts can also be found in current articles— often the source of the most recent figures—or through almanacs, encyclopedias, and other references. If you find information that is a few years old but it is just what you are looking for, check the source. It may be from an agency in Washington that you could contact to obtain updated information.

Chapter Checklist

Sweat the Details

- Have you allowed at least three weeks for developing your speech and blocked off time for it?
- Do you need note cards or full text?
- Have you checked all pronunciations?
- Are you compiling a resource library? Do you know where to find the information you need?

Death by Oratory

A lack of attention to details can undermine an otherwise good speech.

- Don't use a complete text in an intimate setting.
- Don't wait until the last minute to do research. Begin assembling your speaking file as soon as you know you might give a speech.

Chapter Twelve

Working with a Speechwriter

I f you are giving several speeches a week, or are just too pressed with other matters to prepare your own speech, you may need to work with a speechwriter.

Hiring someone to write speeches once raised eyebrows. ("Can't the speaker think of anything interesting to say?") But with the rise to prominence of the professional speechwriter, particularly the presidential speechwriter, there is now widespread acceptance that not all those clever things that come out of the mouths of speech presenters are their own. In fact, certain speechwriters such as presidential pen Peggy Noonan have become almost as celebrated as the people for whom they write.

But how do you go about finding a speechwriter who is compatible with your style? And how do you manage the process in a way that doesn't use more time than it is worth? The management of a free-lance or in-house writer is as challenging as any management process. Unlike other types of management, speechwriting is inherently a creative and therefore messy process. Unless you manage a group of artists or designers, it may be a different management experience from anything else you have encountered.

Don't expect a speechwriter to be able to do everything for you. Sometimes, an experienced writer with little direction from the speaker will come back with an excellent speech. But it won't be your speech. It will be a speech that could be delivered by anyone. The humor, if it exists, will not be your humor. The stories will not be your stories. The words may not be your words. Unless the writer knows you well, you may find yourself delivering a speech that is well written but flat.

WHEN TO HIRE A SPEECHWRITER

You should hire a speechwriter:

- If you have great ideas but have trouble putting words together. Speechwriters can craft a smooth-flowing, entertaining, interesting speech. And you will learn a lot for your next speech.
- If you don't deliver a lot of speeches. Working with a professional can give you greater confidence as you step up to the podium.
- If the speech is very important or your time is very valuable. Speechwriters are not cheap. You can expect to pay a fee of $2,000 or $3,000 for a 20-minute speech, although some accomplished writers earn more than that and some charge less. You will probably be able to find less experienced writers who can do a very good job for much less. Speechwriters do save you some time, and if you are pressed for time, that could be a significant factor in your decision to hire a speechwriter. But the major benefit of hiring a professional is to have someone who knows how to craft a highly polished speech. If you are about to deliver a speech that has great importance for you or your company, having just the right words is critical. There may be no second chance. In this case, the investment may be well worth it.

WHEN NOT TO HIRE A SPEECHWRITER

A speechwriter is probably not the solution if:

- You have accepted a speaking engagement but have drawn a blank on what to say to this audience and want to go fishing for some fresh ideas. The speechwriter may give you some fresh ideas, but they will not be your own. If this is the case, and you are still interested in delivering the speech, make a point to read more about the subject of your speech, or talk to others who are knowledgeable about it. Remember, don't accept engagements for speeches on topics for which you have little experience or enthusiasm. Even a good speechwriter cannot overcome a lack of enthusiasm on the part of the speaker.

- You are so short on time, you can't give five minutes to the project. Working with a speechwriter should cut down on the time you have to spend researching and writing the speech, but it will not reduce the time and attention you have to give to thinking about the speech and rehearsing it. If you can't find time or enthusiasm for these two activities in advance of the speech, then it is better to turn it down.

- You are very uncomfortable with having someone else write for you. If you don't feel right standing up and reading a speechwriter's words, that discomfort will show through. This problem can be mitigated by spending a lot of time with the speechwriter in advance and lots of time revising and rehearsing the speech. No matter where the material came from initially, this process will make it your own.

THE IDEAL SPEECHWRITING PROCESS

A speechwriter is not a manufacturer of speeches but rather a consultant. You don't place your order for a 20-minute speech and pick it up at the take-out window. Speeches are coproduced with the speaker. Find someone with whom you can work and devote enough time to make it work. The key word is *rapport*.

Provide a clear overview of the speech. Have someone call about the audience—know what you are getting into. Set up a summary of audience questions according to the guide in Chapter 9. Set a clear time schedule for the first draft, first revision, and final draft.

Plan to spend at least 20 or 30 minutes discussing the speech proposal with the writer. If you can't tell writers what you want to say, they will be forced to read your mind. Let me warn you, many excellent writers are poor mind readers. Many good speechwriters will refuse to take an assignment unless they are guaranteed direct access to the speaker.

Give speechwriters relevant background materials, including text, audiotapes, or videotapes of past speeches you have delivered. That way, they can more easily write to your pace and rhythm.

Allow at least a few weeks to revise the speech. The first time you work with a writer, you should assume that the speech will go back to the writer for at least one round of revisions. That means you have to give it careful attention and occasionally rethink the whole concept for the speech.

Use speechwriters to help rehearse the speech. Most will not mind the opportunity to fine-tune the delivery of the speech. No one knows it better or has a better sense of how it should sound. Speechwriters can help you bring the speech in line with the text they hear when writing the speech. Writers may recognize sections that do not work for you and thus be able to rewrite them to fit your style. On the other hand, writers may see sections that work particularly well and be able to suggest ways to expand on those themes in the final draft.

THE REAL WORLD

In some cases, speakers have not had a chance to look at the speech drafted by staff or an outside consultant until on the way to the speaking engagement. Sometimes, speakers have to give the speech with little or no time for preparation and rehearsal. This requires great trust, nerves of steel, and tremendous flexibility. Some speakers can pull it off reasonably well. But this is not ideal. It is where mistakes and poor speeches are most likely to turn up.

If, in the crush of business, you find yourself in such a situation, you will have to make do. Sometimes, you have no choice but to have someone else write your speech. Or you don't have much time to devote to the concept and development of the speech. Often, you don't even have the luxury of turning down the speech.

In that case, you need to find the best person to write the speech, giving the writer as much information as you can to start, and trusting that this process will result in an effective presentation. Sometimes, by putting the writer in touch with someone else in the organization with expertise on your topic, the writer can develop a speech that is at least solid, if not tailor-made. Giving the writer an article or paper you have already written on the topic can also save a lot of time.

This may not be perfect, but sometimes it's the only way to give the speech. Any time you can free up to devote to the speech will be time well spent.

HOW TO HIRE A SPEECHWRITER

Hiring a speechwriter is, in many ways, like hiring any other consultant. You want to see their backgrounds, talk to their other clients, and examine samples of their work. One advantage with speechwriters is that you can actually see what they have done for other clients.

The first step is to examine texts. Ask for sample speeches that are as closely related as possible to the type of speech you plan to deliver. If you are planning a 20-minute speech, the text of an introduction will not tell you much about the writer's ability to produce one. If you are looking for a humorous speech, make sure you have a sample that shows the writer's ability to write humor. Sometimes you might find what you are looking for in other writing besides speeches. If the writer has written serious speeches but sidesplitting newspaper columns, you'll have a good shot at putting together a lighthearted speech.

In examining samples, trust your intuition. Don't be dazzled by displays of erudition and pyrotechnics if they don't touch you personally. Don't go for the kind of speech you think you *should* deliver. Look for the kind of speech you would like to hear. If you are entertained and comfortable with the writer's style, it will probably be a good match.

Next, check references or arrange for an initial meeting with the writer. The key point here is chemistry and reliability. You have already established that you like the free-lancer's writing style, but now you need to find out if you like the writer's working style. Is this someone you can be comfortable with? Would you be able to tell the writer that you hate the first draft? Will the writer be able to accept this criticism? Would you be able to open up with this writer and share your personal observations and anecdotes?

Where do you find referrals for speechwriters? Ask colleagues or check through your public relations office for suggestions. Contact speakers whose presentations seemed polished and interesting.

GROWING YOUR OWN

If you or your company have sufficient staff, it might be desirable to cultivate a speechwriter or speechwriters. In the long run, this can be much less expensive than hiring an outside consultant. If there are a few people in your organization with good writing and maybe even speaking skills, they could be good candidates for speechwriting.

Speechwriting is a task that blends well with other activities. An executive assistant or member of the public relations department could often be a good candidate to help with speeches. But remember that writing speeches takes a considerable amount of time. Don't think you can add it to someone's responsibilities without it having an impact on that person's current duties.

Once you have identified someone with promise, make sure you provide the support to help him or her develop this skill. Consider sending the writer to workshops, purchasing a subscription to a speechwriting newsletter, assembling a library of speechwriting resources, and designating time for studying and working at the craft of speechwriting. Also make sure you allow writers time to attend as many speeches as possible to be able to hear the results of their work.

Although you might not find a staff speechwriter of the caliber of a professional consultant, there are several advantages to having an in-house speechwriter. First, the person probably has a much better understanding of the concerns of your organization. An outsider would have to be told about the many issues, positive and negative, that an insider would naturally know. The insider can see connections between information and draw on diverse resources within the organization to which the outsider may not have access.

Second, a staff writer would usually be more available and flexible. Although speech requests would ideally be scheduled far in advance, a last-minute speaking request could be handled more quickly and efficiently in-house.

Third, the staff writer can develop a long-term working relationship with the speaker. If the writer also has other contact with the speaker, this can give the writer access to the speaker's personal experiences, thus enhancing the speech. Rather than relying on the speaker to volunteer suitable stories and examples, as the outsider would be forced to do, the insider can draw these in directly.

Fourth, for the right person, the prospect of writing speeches may be seen as an exciting opportunity to develop a new skill. The resulting motivation can more than make up for the lack of extensive experience.

Finally, it is generally less expensive to have an in-house speechwriter. But the cost savings may come at the expense of quality. If the writer is so overloaded with other assignments that adequate time cannot be devoted to the speech, the quality of the work may suffer. Be sure to allow the writer enough slack time to devote to the speech, and make it clear that it is a priority—if, in fact, it is.

Chapter Checklist

Working with a Speechwriter

- Have you found a writer with whom you can work comfortably?
- Have you clearly defined the project for the writer?
- Have you set aside enough time to meet with the speechwriter to discuss ideas and text?
- If you give many speeches, consider developing the speechwriting abilities of your staff.

Death by Oratory

The speaker has a well-written speech. It is clever. It has ear appeal. It has a good grabber. But the delivery is stiff and unnatural. The speaker has little command of the subject and is only reading the words. It is clear that the speaker bought a great speech but is not delivering one.

- Don't hire a speechwriter if you couldn't write a speech on the topic yourself. It is better to turn down the speaking opportunity.
- Don't expect to hand out the assignment and then carry the speech to the podium. You need to participate in the process.
- Don't expect the speech to be so good you don't have to rehearse. It is still *your* speech.

Chapter Thirteen

Introductions
It Is My Pleasure to Present . . .

S ometimes you are called on to introduce another speaker, either as part of your presentation or if the speaker is a guest of your organization. This requires a different approach than is used in drafting your own remarks. Overall, remain upbeat and complimentary without appearing to be too syrupy. You don't necessarily want the speaker to blush or make apologies, but you do want to make the audience feel like this is someone worth listening to.

The goal of the introduction is to give a context for the speaker's talk. It should discuss the speaker's credentials, where appropriate, the subject of the talk and why it's important to your organization, along with your personal observations ("I first heard Tom speak at . . ."). Never read a biography verbatim. It's cold. It's boring. It's impersonal. Without stealing the speaker's thunder, you can also sometimes give a sense of the broader context for the speech.

For example, when the dean of a major business school introduced U.S. Secretary of Defense Dick Cheney, he discussed the growing importance of geopolitical change in the business school curriculum. He referred to the fundamental changes in world government which are having a profound impact on business. This background helped to stress why Secretary Cheney's insights were especially important at this time and for this audience.

Background. You should give the speaker's name and title and explain why he or she is qualified to speak on this subject. You don't usually have to tell people where the speaker attended grade school, unless that school is where the speech is being given. But if the speaker has a Ph.D. in the subject of the speech, this is a relevant piece of information. Provide as much information as is needed to establish the credibility of the speaker.

Also, make sure you make it clear how the information is related to the topic at hand. For example, instead of saying that the speaker giving a presentation on drug addiction was a journalist for *The New York Times* for a decade, you might say: "Maria saw firsthand the crack houses and drug lords of New York City as a reporter for more than a decade for *The New York Times*."

How well known is the speaker? If the speaker is relatively unknown, you will have to give a fairly detailed account of your guest's background. You will want to touch on every significant point that has bearing on the topic at hand.

If the speaker is very well known, you don't want to drone on about information the audience already knows. You don't have to give President Clinton's life story, for example. But you might find a little-known fact about him that relates his visit to your organization. Probably the most fruitful approach to the introduction at this point is to describe how the invitation came about and why, if you know, the speaker has decided to address your organization.

Where can you get information to introduce speakers? Call their office, or the speaker's bureau who referred them, and ask for an introduction or bio. If speakers have a prepared introduction, this can often be used with little modification. If they don't have a bio, then see if they can send a résumé. If you can't get your hands on a résumé, and the person is relatively well known, you might find information in *Who's Who* and its many cousins. These will be bare bones facts, but it is a start.

You might want to get copies of articles about the speaker or by the speaker. Through them, you could find an interesting story that reveals something about the speaker's character. A short story can be a good introduction.

As mentioned earlier, the best stories, here as in your speech, are those that come from your own experience. If you can say, "I remember the first time I met Joe, he was working on 10 different projects at once. But he still had time to sit down with me and talk about support for our educational foundation. I later found out why. He is the first person in his family to earn his college degree, and it has changed his life. So he has made support of education a priority. Tonight, he will share his insights on what companies need to do to promote better education in American schools."

Don't hog the limelight. In writing a speech, you want to begin with a snappy grabber. For an introduction, a grabber is the last thing you want. Don't do anything to take the spotlight away from the speaker. There is nothing worse than a snappy and exciting introduction followed by a mediocre speech. With a less entertaining intro, the speaker may have had a fighting chance. But after the bright lights of the flashy intro, the audience is blinded. Your role is not to be the speaker, just to be the introducer.

The only way to focus attention on the speaker without competing with the speaker is to tell an interesting story about your guest. This way you can be entertaining, but the focus is still squarely on the speaker. You earn points as an introducer, not by making yourself look clever, but by making your speaker look clever and qualified. If you know a good story, you are all set. If you can find one by digging around a bit, you are also all set. If you don't have the time or inclination to dig one up, there is not too much lost. Just give a straightforward introduction clearly stating the speaker's qualification to discourse on the topic at hand.

At the end of the introduction, introduce the speaker. Don't trail off. Simply end with the presenter's name. Then the audience and speaker know that you are finished and it is time for the speaker to take over.

Most of all, be brief. If you take more than a minute or two to introduce the speaker, you've spent too long. The audience did not come to hear you speak. As introducer, you are like the waiter who seats guests at the table. If you hang around too long, you are an annoyance. They want to put their order in and get to the main course. Do what you have to do. Then get out of the way.

Chapter Checklist

Introductions

- Have you identified the speaker's name and title?
- Have you made a strong case for why the speaker is an authority on this subject?
- Have you included an anecdote, if available?
- Have you shared with the audience a common, personal experience you've had with the guest?

Death by Oratory

A host once made a fairly long introduction to George V. Grune, chairman and chief executive officer of the Reader's Digest Association. Grune began his remarks:

> Thank you, Bob, for your kind and comprehensive introduction. It ran longer than what our editors usually accept for the "Personal Glimpses" section of *Reader's Digest*, but I won't quibble.[14]

It is not uncommon for a speaker to refer to the introducer in his opening (as we discussed in Chapter 2). It helps make a bridge. But don't make the length of your introduction so noticeable, no matter how wonderful the words, that it deserves mention by the speaker. Other pitfalls to avoid:

- Don't make the introduction so flashy that it overshadows the speaker.
- Don't give all the pointless details of the speaker's biography. Stick to the facts that relate to the topic at hand.
- Never *ever* read a biography or résumé verbatim—especially not the part that "the speaker is married and has two children" unless it is absolutely relevant to the speech.

II

PERFORMANCE

"The play's the thing."

William Shakespeare

S howtime!
    You've included all the essential elements of a successful presentation in your preparations. You know the audience. You're to speak on a subject that's important to *you and the audience.* You've got your grabber. You've built in your road maps and signs. Your material has structure. It's got technique. It has ear appeal.

Now, it's time to go on!

The best written material in the hands of a poor performer can quickly be converted into the worst written material. Conversely, a poorly written script in the hands of a quality performer can come alive.

I was at NBC when one of Major League Baseball's most innovative executives—the late Branch Rickey—died. It was Branch Rickey who broke color barriers by bringing the late Jackie Robinson from the old Negro baseball leagues to the then Brooklyn

Dodgers, opening up unlimited opportunities to talented minority players.

My boss assigned me the job of writing a eulogy suitable for on-air reading by one of our sportscasters. Because I was a baseball fan and a Dodger one at that, I was very familiar with the contributions of Branch Rickey. I liked him. I liked what he stood for. I loved the Dodgers and greatly admired the talent and most of all the courage of Jackie Robinson. Knowing the story, I wrote what I thought was a fairly solid review of Branch Rickey's achievements.

But nothing prepared me for the powerful, dramatic, emotional, and effective way my words were communicated by a professional sportscaster. The enunciation, the pauses, the emphasis, and the emotion added that human quality that made the listeners feel. They felt the enormity of Branch Rickey's achievements. They felt the tragedy of his death.

That's your job as a speechgiver. To make the audience feel. Not just listen. Not just think. But feel. Become moved.

The elements of a successful performance include:

- Practice, practice, practice.
- Arriving early.
- Being animated and using gestures.
- Reading the eyes of the audience.
- Energy and enthusiasm.

It's showtime!

Chapter Fourteen

Rehearse!
It's Good for Your Nerves

There are all sorts of miracle cures for sweating hands and chattering teeth. Among the most intriguing:

- Imagine that the entire audience is stark naked.
- Take 10 deep breaths.
- Do deep-knee bends.
- Before going on, close your eyes and imagine yourself by a babbling brook or in another favorite place.
- Bend down and put your head between your knees.
- Go for a five-minute walk.
- Kiss your lucky rabbit's foot or four-leaf clover.

You name it, it has probably been tried. Some people swear by their favorite nerve-calming technique. But the best way to achieve calmness is the old-fashioned way—earn it, through hard work, preparation, and practice.

Every new experience—whether it's starting a new job, learning to ride a bike, or giving a speech—is most frightening the first time. It is only with the confidence gained through repetition and practice that the nervousness subsides. It may not go away completely. For many people, it may always be there in the background. But it won't be in charge of the speech. You will be.

Fear comes from the unknown. So get to know your speech, intimately. Know your audience. Know what it feels like to step up to a microphone, because you have practiced it. Make your speech so familiar that you could care less about it. Tear it apart and analyze it like a frog in a biology lab. Explore every nook and cranny where invisible demons may be hiding. Make your speech an old friend. Then walk arm in arm up to the podium and introduce your speech to the audience. Who could be afraid in the presence of an old friend? Then, if you need to go into a yoga position before you step up to the podium, do it. Do whatever it takes to calm your nerves. But the best defense, in this case, is a strong offense. So I have just one offbeat piece of advice: Say this mantra as you gear up for your performance. Practice. Practice. Practice. Shantih. Shantih. Shantih. (Translation: Peace. Peace. Peace.) Keep saying this. And follow the advice. And practice until you are so bored with the speech you couldn't possibly be afraid of it.

HOW MUCH REHEARSAL IS ENOUGH?

I remember riding in a car with actor George Peppard years ago. He was a spokesman for one of my clients, and we were on our way to a television interview. During the ride over to the studio we were discussing a film director who insisted on lots of extra takes.

I had suggested that perhaps it was overkill, that these additional takes were needlessly driving up the cost of movies, and that "good" was "good enough." The actor quickly turned to me and sharply disagreed, suggesting there was no substitute for perfection. Evidently for George Peppard, good enough was clearly not "good enough." Bravo, George.

Perhaps the answer lies somewhere in between, although I must confess that I find myself coming down more and more on the side of preparation and perfection. Some people can just show up, start talking, make a lot of sense, and leave an enormous emotional impact. Sportscaster Howard Cosell was one of them. It's been said that all he would do when he showed up at the studio for his network radio show was ask his producer how much time he needed to fill. Then he'd launch into his story and at exactly the right moment reach his dramatic conclusion. That's talent.

Few of us—and I'm certainly not one of them—have that gift. Most of us, like Thomas Edison, find that genius "is 1 percent inspiration and 99 percent perspiration." Perspiration in speech-making means preparation (you can sweat before the speech or sweat during the speech, your choice). The Israelis, known to have one of the best fighting forces in the world, tell their new trainees, "The more you sweat here, the less likely you are to bleed there." To me, preparation is spelled R-E-H-E-A-R-S-A-L!

Many a night in my hotel room the day before a presentation I would recite my speech out loud. If I was using slides, I would ask the A/V people to have a carousel available to me in my room so I could make certain my visuals were smoothly coordinated into my speech.

Ideally, if you have someone who can listen to you rehearse and give you feedback, this is the best arrangement. Then you can "hear" the speech through other ears. You can also look at your audience of one and assess how your words are affecting your listener. That is sometimes harder to do during the course of the speech.

Rehearsing out loud accomplishes several things. By reciting your words, again and again, you firmly implant those words in your mind's ear, easily recallable when you're up on your feet. You also make those words so familiar by rehearsing that they're difficult to forget.

Some words, even those you are quite comfortable with in type, may give you trouble when it comes to pronunciation. If you are using proper names, you might need to look up pronunciations or ask someone how to pronounce them and note that in your text.

You can also work on your timing and mark places where you need to be sure to pause. Where should your voice rise, where should it soften? When should you move forward deliberately, and when should you stop for a moment to allow a point to sink in? Your rehearsal may be the only time you have to listen to the speech in a relaxed setting.

Rehearsing out loud also affords you the opportunity to assess whether or not what you're saying makes any sense. If it doesn't sound terribly convincing to you, it's not likely to sway others. Therefore, rehearsing out loud helps you modify and strengthen your positions so your material has more substance, more believability.

One other component of rehearsal needs to be mentioned: anticipating likely post-presentation questions and developing answers to those questions. In Part III, we discuss some of the types of questions you might face and how you might respond to them.

As part of your preparation, it's a good idea to play the role of skeptic. Pretend you are an investigative reporter from a respected news-gathering organization assigned to cover your speech, then interview yourself after your delivery. In that role, draw up a list of the toughest, most difficult, perhaps even mean-spirited questions you can possibly think up. Then make certain you have answers to those questions.

Lastly, in advance of your speech, sit down with your secretary, your assistant, your spouse, and/or your youngster, and let them play devil's advocate. Have them ask you those difficult-bordering-on-outrageous questions, and let them add any of their own. Then answer them. You might even videotape or audiotape the exercise. During the playback, it'll be easy to ascertain where answers need to be modified or specifics need to be added for documentation.

ARRIVE EARLY

Just some of the things I have learned by arriving early to my presentations:

- A 3/4-inch video tape will not play in a 1/2-inch deck.
- A 1/2-inch videocassette tape will not track in a 3/4-inch playback unit.
- Overhead transparencies are useless in a carousel.
- A flip chart without a wide-tip, color felt marker is a poor visual aid.

- Thursday is not Friday (I once arrived late on Wednesday, thinking I was scheduled to present on Thursday, when the actual day for my presentation was Friday).

- Fort Leonard Wood is not Lake of the Ozarks, Missouri (where I was actually scheduled to speak—but my travel agent inadvertently sent me 150 miles away).

There is no substitute for being there. I'm told that the Sunday before the 1992 Democratic Convention Senator Bill Bradley went over to an empty Madison Square Garden and rehearsed from the podium out loud before delivering his speech the next night.

The amount of miscommunication between inviter and presenter is truly amazing. In spite of all the reconfirming letters and follow-up phone calls, things can—and often do—go wrong.

The only way I know of correcting them is to arrive early. Get there before the audience does. Check out the mike. Nothing is as amateurish—and boring—as a speaker whose first words are "Can everyone in the back of the room hear me okay?" Truly a rotten grabber at best, and to me a tip off that there's probably little original material in what's about to follow.

You should not have to ask if everyone can hear you. You should know because you yourself checked out the audio level before the audience began to arrive.

Arrive early to arrange the room to your liking. Does the setting call for a group of round tables (good for work sessions and team exercises)? Or do you prefer classroom styling—tables and chairs set one row after another (good for work sessions without team exercises)? Or perhaps a simple auditorium style? Arrive early to set the appropriate stage.

Arrive early to adjust the lighting. If it is too bright to see your slides or overheads, then find out how to turn it down. If it is too dark at the lectern to read your remarks, then see if you can find a light.

Arrive early to preset and precheck your audiovisual equipment. You want them arranged so you can easily access them without creating unnecessary pauses or interruptions in your delivery, and you certainly want to make sure they work.

Arrive early to heighten your self-assurance, your sense of confidence that everything is in good working order and laid out just the way you want it.

Arrive early so that once you've attended to all these matters, you'll still have most of your time to focus on your performance to follow.

Arrive early to thoroughly familiarize yourself with every aspect of your environment. The more comfortable you feel, the more confident you will appear, and the better the speech will be.

Chapter Checklist

Rehearse!

- Have you rehearsed your speech to the point that you feel completely comfortable with it?
- Can you rehearse in front of others to get feedback?
- If you are using visuals, can you arrange for equipment to rehearse the night before?
- Have you marked your speech for places to pause and make emphasis?
- Have you anticipated possible questions and developed answers to them?
- Have you made plans to arrive early?
- Have you arranged to go into the auditorium or meeting room in advance of the speech? Did you check with the organizers to make sure you will have access to the room? Have you established contact with an A/V person?
- If you are going to a strange place, allow extra time to scout out the location and prepare yourself.
- Is there time to run through your entire presentation in the room where you will speak?
- Will you be able to test out equipment before the start of the program?

Death by Oratory

A young Arizona school admissions director was sent to give his first speech as part of a panel at the annual meeting of a national association of independent schools in Georgia. He hadn't prepared, didn't rehearse, and was unsure about what he wanted to say. To make matters worse, he had had almost nothing to eat before going on stage. Despite these drawbacks, his presentation made quite an impression on the audience, and the paramedics.

Less than a minute into his talk, he fainted and was down for the count. An ambulance arrived and brought him back to consciousness. Clearly, he didn't get to finish his remarks.

Years later, he continues to give speeches, but with a slightly different approach. He recalls that there were several silver linings and lessons from the experience. The first is that he is now less afraid of problems at speaking engagements. He had lived through the worst-case scenario and survived. What else could go wrong? He also learned to make sure he was well prepared and well fed before giving a presentation. The last silver lining is that now he has a great story to tell at the start of his speeches.

- Don't think that by reading the speech through you are rehearsing it. At the very least, read it aloud to yourself. Or, better yet, read it to someone else.

- Don't schedule your preparation time so tightly that you leave no time for rehearsing.

- Don't think that you can go on without a rehearsal. Even a professional actor wouldn't do that. The most dangerous and nerve-racking thing you can do in preparing for a speech is to put off rehearsing it.

- Don't assume that *anything* will be the way it is promised to be, unless you see it for yourself. Don't expect to get any special assistance on your journey because you are headed to a presentation. Assume the heaviest traffic, the worst blizzards, the slowest taxis.

- Don't schedule yourself so tightly that you have no time to get to the event early. Add an extra hour or two to your calendar. Then bring along work to do if you end up with downtime. You'll be more relaxed working at the site of your presentation than wondering if you will arrive on time.

Chapter Fifteen

Be Animated
Gestures and Energy

It was a gesture that transformed a nation. In 1783, the Continental Congress was powerless to collect taxes, and the military officers of the Continental Army were growing increasingly discontented about unpaid wages and lost pensions. There was talk among the officers of using force to compel the states to pay their federal debts.

George Washington called a meeting of the officers to try to prevent an uprising in the new republic. He exhorted them not "to open the floodgates of civil discord." But his words fell on deaf ears.

Then Washington remembered he had brought a reassuring letter from a congressman. He reached into his pocket, pulled out the letter, and then stared blankly at the paper in his hands for a few minutes, helplessly.

Then he pulled out something only his closest confidants had seen him wear, a pair of eyeglasses. As he looked up at the audience, he said, "Gentlemen, you will permit me to put on my spectacles, for I have not only grown gray but almost blind in the service of my country." Soldiers wept. The gathering was transformed. The rebellion was quelled.[15]

Sometimes a simple gesture can say volumes. And if a gesture is accompanied by the right words, it can have an even more powerful effect. Something as simple as removing your glasses, looking straight at the audience, and gesturing with your hands can make a dramatic impact on your audience.

On the other hand, gestures can also dampen the effect of the speech. If a speaker is talking about openness and communication but has his arms crossed against his chest, his body language is contradicting his words.

How you look may be as important as what you say and will undoubtedly have an impact on how people react to you and your message. In talking about how critical this is for a television interview, a friend at one of the television networks once suggested that "how you look on camera may be as important as what you say on mike."

The same is true—although arguably to a lesser degree—when making a presentation. How you stand, what you do with your hands and the rest of your body, and where you look will either add to or detract from your performance.

We mainly communicate with our eyes and our hands. Hands should not be extended the full length of the lectern, clutching the far corners. This suggests fear and apprehension, so much fear that you need a life preserver (the lectern) to hold onto. Ideally, you should stand about a foot away from the lectern.

Keep your hands close to your body. Keep them up. If you must hold onto the lectern, hold on with only one hand and use one of the corners closest to you, freeing the other hand for gestures and turning pages. Stand straight.

MAKING THE FIST AN EXCLAMATION POINT

Speaking of gestures, they play a key role in your presentation where some degree of animation and punctuation on your part is called for. You shouldn't be as animated as the overzealous used-car or electronics salespeople depicted in some television commercials. But movements that coincide with the ebb and flow of your material will help you emphasize key points.

By way of example, I recently observed a skilled political communicator make a fist with his right hand. In one quick motion, he brought the fist down, just brushing the top of his notes and crossing his body, ending up near his left shoulder, signaling a hand over his heart. He did this as he said to the audience, "And if elected, by God, I'm not going to be so extravagant with your money that we continue to spend our way into a depression."

Such gestures, used sparingly and appropriately, effectively underscore points a presenter is making. You might even want to program some of them into your presentation.

The politician could also have employed a more subtle technique to underscore that portion of his text. He could have paused, looked up at the audience, removed his glasses, and spoken his words firmly, but not quite as emphatically. Or he could have paused, removed his glasses, walked out from behind the lectern, and delivered that line directly to the attendees.

Three different gestures. Three different approaches. Each would work. The key is to pick out the one that works best for you.

Sometimes the context of the speech will determine the most appropriate gestures to use. For example, a small group will be able to see subtle gestures such as facial expressions and shifts in posture. A large audience will need clearer and broader gestures such as sweeps of the hand or walking out from behind the lectern.

PREGNANT PAUSES

Crescendo! Allegro! Fortissimo! Musical terms to be sure. Just as there are movements in music, so too should there be vocal variety in a speech; peaks and pauses. Without them, it's like listening to a symphony in one movement. After a while, the listener gets bored. Musician Artur Schnabel said, "The notes I handle not better than many pianists. But the pauses between the notes—ah, that is where the art resides."[16]

We all crave variety: different places, different people, different things. This is especially true in a speech where the audience may be looking for an excuse to tune out. By giving the audience such vocal variety, you give them a reason to hang in.

Consider some of the most popular concerts, symphonies, or even songs. If they start with a bang (Beethoven's *Fifth*), that bang is usually followed by a soft and tender passage. Conversely, a gently, understated opening invariably results in a buildup toward a resounding close.

Think of your material as a piece of music that needs to be orchestrated and scored. Some parts may require a soft voice and a slow pace, while others will need a louder tone and a faster pace. The material should dictate which of these two is more appropriate.

How do you achieve vocal variety?

Remember, first impressions count. Sometimes speakers, anxious about delivering their remarks, rush right into their text rather than savoring the moment. It is a mistake to think that listeners come to hear words delivered as quickly as possible. They come for the performance. And the performance is as much in the silences as it is in the speaking.

When you're first introduced, upon arriving at the podium or your point of delivery, take a break, wait a beat. Scan the room for about five seconds, eyeball to eyeball. Pick out a friendly face or two. Smile. Then deliver your grabber—again, eyeball to eyeball—without notes.

Unless you pause for 10 minutes, the audience will stay with you. The pause will actually build increased expectation and potential acceptance for your opening words. And if you hit them with a strong grabber, the increased expectation and attention will be well justified.

This will engage your audience. It will involve them. It will help separate people from their own concerns and more than likely immerse them in yours.

Perhaps the most powerful form of oral punctuation is the pause. Yet many presenters feel that if they're not talking continually, they're not communicating. A moment of silence, a brief halt to the verbiage to allow it to settle in and be digested, can be a potent weapon in the arsenal of any communicator.

Again, the material will dictate when such a break is appropriate. My own observation is that most presenters overaccelerate their rate of delivery, making it difficult for audiences to stay in step.

One way to curb overacceleration is to make certain you enunciate every letter of every word.

So err, here, on the side of conservatism. Speak enthusiastically. But speak slowly, varying your pace just enough with pauses and perhaps sprinkled with some rapid-fire phrases to provide your audience with enough vocal variety to sustain their interest.

ENERGY LEVEL

It has been suggested that nothing begins to happen until something is sold, and the essence of good selling—in addition to knowing what the potential customer needs—is enthusiasm.

The same is true in speechmaking. Speaking is selling. You're selling a concept. You're selling a product. You're selling a service. You're selling your organization's capabilities. Most importantly, you're selling yourself.

People buy sincerity. People buy integrity. People buy longevity (your track record), and people buy energy. They buy from those sellers whose energy level is high, who are driven by conviction and truly believe in what they're promoting.

Therefore, if you want to win audiences over to your thinking and gain their support, you must elevate your emotions.

Not to a feverish pitch. Not to the point of shouting. But rather, to the level that confirms to the audience that you totally believe in your material.

Early in my career, I used to write the word *enthusiasm* on the front page of my speech. It was a cue to myself to push my energy lever forward a notch.

There is a danger of becoming overly enthusiastic and perhaps intimidating or irritating an audience. Recently, I noticed my voice level elevating almost to the point of shouting. Usually, aside from hearing myself, the first clue is when I notice a member or two of the audience looking away from me when I seek to establish eye contact. That clue, plus hearing myself, causes me to moderate my voice level.

There is evidently a fine line between an overly enthusiastic presentation and one that's underenergized. That fine line is different for each of us. But in general, I'd say most presentations suffer from a lack of excitement.

The bottom line? Find a comfortable level of enthusiasm that makes you sound interesting and believable. The level you seek is probably slightly higher than your current delivery level.

Chapter Checklist

Be Animated

- Where are appropriate places in your speech to add meaningful gestures?
- Have you made a note to pause before delivering your grabber and to keep your energy level up?
- Where else can you add pauses or emphasis in your speech?
- Remember to stand back from the lectern with at least one hand free for gesturing.
- Have you paid attention to your posture and gestures during your rehearsals? What needs to be changed?
- Ask a friend or colleague to observe your gestures while you are rehearsing or delivering a speech. What are the weaknesses of your style? What are the strengths? How can you enhance the strengths and overcome the weaknesses?

Death by Oratory

If you act like a relic, they may haul you off to a museum. If you moonwalk onto the podium and whirl like Michael Jackson, you may get a contract with MTV but no one will be able to hear a word you say. So don't go to extremes:

- Don't rely on the power of your words alone to carry the day. Add some life to them.
- Don't be stone-faced and rigid. No one wants to listen to a statue.
- Don't wave your hands like a lunatic. Your listeners may fear for their lives.
- Don't keep your hands in your pockets jiggling change.
- Don't drape yourself over the lectern with your hands grabbing the corners closest to the audience. Rather, keep one hand free for gestures, the other free for changing pages.
- Don't staple pages; instead, slide them across from side to side.
- Don't fold your arms in front of your chest (this suggests anger, hostility, or combativeness).
- Don't fold your hands behind you (as if you're about to go ice skating).
- Don't sway. Don't rock.

Chapter Sixteen

Read the Audience
The Eyes Have It

A uthor and management consultant Peter Drucker once commented, "The most important thing in communication is to hear what isn't being said." Your audience doesn't have an opportunity to speak to you during your presentation, but if you listen closely, you can "hear what isn't being said." Audience members speak with their eyes. To hear them, you have to look at them.

Years ago, I was invited to attend a presentation being given by the late Sam Levenson. For those of you who don't recognize the name, Sam Levenson was a humorist and author who wrote and spoke warmly about the poor but loving and supportive home in which he was raised. He was a frequent guest on radio and television talk shows, and he was considered a terrific speaker. So much so that when one of my friends suggested we go hear him that evening, I was receptive.

I had also met Sam Levenson when he appeared as a guest on a talk show I once produced for NBC. So I knew him. I liked him.

We arrived early. Rather than an auditorium, Mr. Levenson was speaking at a theatrical club in Manhattan. The room was set up with roughly 12 round tables with 10 chairs at each. Because I greatly admired him and because I arrived early, I chose a front seat at the table closest to the podium.

To my great disappointment, not once throughout his talk did Sam Levenson look at me. He looked to my left. He looked to my right. He looked over my head. But not at me. I felt slighted. I felt rejected to the point where I became fidgety and uncomfortable. At times, I tuned out and found myself hoping the evening would soon end.

Making eye contact with as many people in the audience as possible is an essential ingredient in any successful presentation. Years ago, some speech teachers used to recommend that presenters pick a spot over the heads of the assembly and talk to it. Poor advice!

Members of the audience want to know you care enough about them to talk directly to them. Therefore, it's incumbent on presenters to speak to the eyes in the audience.

Here's how. The end of each sentence is an ideal spot to stop, look up from your material, seek out the eyes of several members of the listening audience, and embrace those eyes for a second or two. But that's not the only time to establish eye contact. Throughout your talk—at the top of each sentence, in the middle of the sentence, and as already mentioned, at the end—scan eyes. Even if it slows the pace of your presentation, scan eyes.

Most importantly, avoid the trap of reading a speech verbatim so that your eyes are mainly buried in your material. Nothing is deadlier.

Years ago, I was in the audience when the CEO of a Fortune top-five U.S. corporation gave a 45-minute dissertation on the consumer movement. This CEO was attractive, articulate, and a newsmaker. He could have been interesting. But he read his speech word for word, burying his eyes in his text. It was deadly. The audience tuned out. People clearly became restless. Many left the room.

I thought to myself, that executive would have better served his audience by handing out an advance copy of his text and then hosting a question and answer session. He probably would have gotten a more positive listener reaction and his appearance would have been more meaningful for all.

The main objective of establishing meaningful eye contact is to keep the audience interested and involved. But a by-product is feedback. It's almost like an instant report card. By looking up frequently and meaningfully, you can gauge whether an audience is keeping pace or restless. If you do ascertain some tuning out, you can adapt by cutting your material and moving on to other information certain to engage them and recapture their interest. Or you can even shorten it, end it, and go to the Q&A earlier.

As already suggested, the best place to establish eye contact is at the outset. Memorize your opening lines so they are delivered right to the eyes of the audience. This will immediately engage them and lock them onto your every word.

To maintain and preserve that relationship, use the "look up" approach. From scanning to staring to embracing, the more eye contact you build into your presentation, the more successful that presentation will become.

IMPROVISE

A traveler in Warsaw in the 1970s was headed to the train station to catch an early morning express to Krakow. She went to the spot where the station was supposed to be, according to the map. It was an empty lot. She stopped passing pedestrians, and in halting Polish, asked where the station was. They said, right here. She eventually found that the train was running underground. A few weeks before she had arrived, the station had been torn down.

Giving a speech is like traveling in a foreign country: You don't know the terrain until you see it, and you can't be sure the people you are talking to will speak your language. You have a great script for your speech but you notice that the man in the middle of the first row is nodding off. A woman on the other side of the room is doodling on her notepad. You feel the audience slipping away.

The speech, which sounded so good in the privacy of your own living room, now has turned pasty and bland in your mouth. The words that flowed like Shakespearean dialogue have slowed to a trickle. You can feel you are losing the audience. There is no time to stop the music and rewrite the speech. What you need to do is to improvise.

WHAT ARE THEY TELLING YOU?

Unless they are hurling fermenting vegetables at the podium, your audience has few direct ways of communicating their displeasure with your speech. To know how your audience is reacting to your speech, you have to read them. As suggested earlier, the ideal place to do this is at the end of a sentence. Stop for a moment. Look up at your audience. Take their temperature. It usually isn't too hard to tell how your audience feels if you look at them.

Several signs will tell you whether or not you're connecting—whether or not you're getting through

- If you see folded arms, they're feeling a bit hostile. (Of course, it could just mean the room is cold.)
- If there's lots of fidgeting and other movement, a mass exodus may be at hand.
- If you look into someone's eyes and he or she avoids your gaze, you may be losing that person.
- If you see closed eyelids, no doubt about it, you've lost your audience.

Recently, during a presentation, I noticed that every time I'd look at one person in the audience, she would look down. I immediately knew I was losing her. Then I listened to myself. My energy level was much too high, to the point that I was nearly shouting at my audience. I caught myself and moderated my tone to make it more conversational. A few moments later when I again looked at the young woman, I was happy to note that instead of averting her eyes, she embraced mine with her own.

I lowered my voice. She raised her eyes.

BEWARE OF FRIENDLY FACES

Seeking out hostile listeners is exactly the opposite of the advice that some speech trainers give. They say to seek out those friendly eyes and latch onto them like a piece of driftwood on a stormy sea.

Some speakers, especially those just beginning, may need to do this. They may not be comfortable seeking out listeners who are unhappy. A scowling face could make them lose heart. If you are feeling a bit thin-skinned, maybe you should seek out a few approving sets of eyes or plant a few in the front row. But it is preferable to seek out lost sheep, as difficult as it may be to bring them back into the fold.

I remember a colleague giving a presentation to a hostile audience of potential clients. There were six people at the presentation, and five of them were scowling with their arms crossed. But that sixth one was smiling broadly and hanging on every word. The presenter took heart and concentrated on that one friendly face, giving his all to the presentation. Even though the odds were not in his favor, at least if he could convince this one listener, he had a shot at getting the account.

After the presentation, as the dissatisfied five shuffled out, the sixth came up and congratulated the presenter. Then he introduced himself. He was from the presenter's company, not the client firm. He had decided to sit in on the presentation.

The moral is that preaching to the already converted will not win anyone over to your cause.

YOU'RE LOSING THEM: WHAT DO YOU DO?

If you notice the audience is slipping away, you might be able to make minor changes to your delivery to bring them back, as I did in the instance above. Sometimes it calls for more drastic measures.

You might need to take an especially long pause, or even shorten your presentation and go right to the questions and answers.

This is a delicate moment. If you jump from your prepared text, you may find yourself wandering aimlessly in the wilderness, looking to find yourself again. But if you can think fast and segue into a more lively section, skip over the dry spots until you come to a story or image that has more power.

You might look for a spot to interject a question. If you have a section of the speech that begins with a statement, sometimes adding a simple "Why? I'll tell you why" transition can bring people back.

A lost audience can also be a sign that they are not following your road maps. You might need to find a suitable break where you can review where you have taken them and reiterate where you are going. This can help to get them back on track.

Or you might not move away from your prepared speech at all. Instead, you can put renewed energy into it or tone it down. The fading audience is a sign that you need to renew your efforts to connect with them. You need to reach a little farther. Just like a lover's quarrel is not a sign of the end of a relationship. But it takes some mending fences, some roses, some extra effort.

This is where you improvise.

The most important point is to do something. If you notice your audience slipping away and don't do anything, you will lose more and more of them. It will be a negative cycle. Any action is better than nothing.

Chapter Checklist

Read the Audience

- Do you engage the eyes of your audience? Do you look them directly in the eye during the opening and grabber and look up at the end of each sentence?
- Read the eyes of your audience to determine if they are still following:
  - Are people averting their eyes, crossing their arms, or otherwise signaling their disapproval?
- If so, you need to adjust your speech by:
  - Speeding up or slowing down.
  - Increasing energy or throttling back.
  - Injecting questions.

- Reestablishing road maps.
- Inserting a pause until there is quiet.
- Cutting to a more interesting part of the presentation.
- Moving right into the Q&A.

Death by Oratory

An executive speaker at a workshop had his back to the audience, reading from his overheads. He couldn't tell that his listeners were fidgeting. He couldn't tell that they were bored. He was too busy reading his own words to read the audience. Don't do that.

• Don't bury your nose in your remarks. If you don't look up, you have no way of knowing if the audience is still there. Even if you don't know the speech well, at least look out to the audience at the end of every sentence.

• Don't stare at a point in the back of the room. The point is not listening to your speech. Scan for eyes. Seek them out. Read them. Find more.

• Don't look aside when you connect with the eyes of a listener. Determine what's there—delight or a desperate plea for mercy. And act on the information.

III

POST–PRESENTATION: CHAIRING THE Q&A

"It is better to know some of the questions than all of the answers."

James Thurber

Y ou've made it through the speech. With any luck, the audience still has a strong pulse and may remember a few key phrases from your discourse. You can be proud as you wipe your brow, take a sip of water, and bask in the well-deserved applause. But you're not out of the woods yet. Now comes what may be your greatest adventure: the Q&A.

Ordeal or opportunity? With the right preparation, the question-and-answer period following a recitation is a wonderful chance to reinforce the main points made during the speech. The audience welcomes the change of format from presentation to conversation.

This part of the presentation calls for a whole different mindset, a different set of approaches, and a different form of preparation. If the speech is a symphony, this is jazz. If the speech is Shakespeare, this is improv. If the speech is a sermon, this is a classroom discussion. Your speech requires that you perform well, but the Q&A requires that you think fast on your feet, and most important of all, that you listen.

Some people who are excellent speakers have trouble with the spontaneity of the open questions. Some who are great at fielding questions struggle through their prepared remarks. The key thing is to know where you fall on the spectrum of abilities. Most inherent weaknesses can be overcome or compensated for by preparation.

In this final part, we'll analyze the kinds of questions you might encounter, and we'll suggest several techniques for successfully chairing the post-presentation Q&A, including:

• Handling debates.
• Using names.
• Repeating the question.
• Making friends.

Chapter Seventeen

Anticipate a Variety of Questions

Having sat in on many speeches and many interviews, and as both a student of—and a former member of—the journalistic profession, I have, over the years, cataloged a variety of question categories. I'd like to point them out, then suggest ways to handle them:

- Open-ended questions.
- Close-ended questions.
- Hypothetical questions.
- Questions that paraphrase your remarks.
- Dart thrower questions.
- Relate questions.
- Worst-case questions.
- Machine-gunner questions.

Let's look at each of these types of questions and ascertain how best to handle them.

The types of questions and answers presented here may be more hostile than the ones you are likely to face. We use many examples from media briefings, but these same techniques can be applied just as easily to responding to business questions. While most of the questions pitched at you after a presentation will not be this challenging, it is best to prepare for the worst. Friendly questions can be responded to using these same general approaches, and are, in general, much easier to respond to effectively.

John F. Kennedy's press briefings, cited extensively below, are a fine example of using humor and wit to respond to (and sometimes avoid) questions. His techniques and, more important, his overall approach to the process offer a good model for speakers in responding to questions.

The two most common forms of questions you'll likely be asked are close-ended and open-ended questions. Both present opportunities for you to reiterate an important message made in your speech.

CLOSE–ENDED VERSUS OPEN–ENDED

The close-ended question is distinguished by its answer, in that it only requires a simple yes or no. It's probably asked more often than the open-ended question, which requires a less specific but more elaborate response. Attorneys and journalists are learning to ask more open-ended questions because the answers are longer, allowing more opportunity for follow-up or exploration. This is clearly more beneficial to attorneys and journalists seeking to uncover wrongdoing or attempting to uncover the truth.

The expansive answer afforded by the open-ended question allows the one asking it to follow up on the material introduced by the answer. For example:

Close-ended question

Does your company have an engineer on staff?

Open-ended question

Could you describe your organizational capabilities?

As suggested, either the open- or close-ended question gives you a chance to review and amplify the messages contained in your recitation.

Inasmuch as the open-ended form is an obvious entree into reiteration, let's focus on the "yes or no" form to see how you can turn it into an opportunity.

There's a formula for doing so. It starts by first answering the question with the required yes or no. Next, add an amplification, giving a reason for the yes or no. Having answered the question directly and completely, you could stop here and go on to the next question. But that would be like punting on first down. With four chances to gain 10 yards, you wouldn't want to punt here. Rather, make the question work for you by making a transition statement from what was asked to the point you want to reinforce, then go into a reiteration of your message.

Here are some sample transition phrases:

- I should also mention . . .
- We should also be discussing . . .
- I'd like to point out . . .
- Let me point out something else that's relevant here . . .
- Let me change directions for a moment . . .
- I should also remind you . . .
- That question brings something else to mind related to our discussion . . .

Then, once you've made your transition, you've created an opportunity for yourself to remind the audience of the focal points made in your presentation. This formula allows you to convert a close-ended question into the more ideal open-ended one so you can repeat your messages.

But keep your message brief here. If you spend 15 seconds answering the question and ramble on for five minutes making your own point, the audience will think you are not listening. There are few things more annoying than speakers who do not answer the questions they are asked, but instead answer the questions they *wish* they had been asked. Use discretion, but make your point.

HYPOTHETICAL QUESTIONS

The most often asked type of question is the hypothetical or "what will you do if . . ." question. It's the staple of the media diet and journalists frequently force politicians to deal with it.

Supposedly, President Franklin Delano Roosevelt refused to. When he became president, he told the press he was setting out one ground rule: He would not answer any questions requiring him to speculate on any issue. I'm told he never violated his rule. Clearly, that's one option. Another option is denial, pure and simple, that the hypothetical possibility exists. It is a hard position to argue with and can show your clear determination not to let the hypothetical scenario come to pass. When President Kennedy was asked what he intended to do about a proposed tax cut, he first went into a fairly detailed explanation of the issues involved. This wasn't what the reporter had wanted.

Reporter:
What I meant was, what do you plan to do if you don't get the tax cut?
John F. Kennedy:
I plan to get the tax cut.

End of debate. The audience laughs. You laugh. Even your questioner may laugh. This is a much better response than hedging and tracing out a wide range of scenarios that you hope will not come to pass. No uncomfortable silences. No giving away your alternate positions to your opponents. That's all there is to it.

If you are an economic forecaster, you have no choice but to deal with hypotheticals. The rest of us usually have a choice. If, in fact, you're comfortable with the mythical scenario depicted in the question and have anticipated such eventualities to the point where you've developed specific responses, and if sharing those is in your best interest, then proceed. By all means, answer the hypothetical question asked.

If, on the other hand, this type of question can be troublesome and at some point down the road your answer could come back to haunt you, then it's appropriate to pass. Vice President Dan Quayle caused a stir when he was asked a question about how he would respond if his daughter were to tell him she wanted to have an abortion. He was caught between his public pro-life stance and his paternal role of supporting his daughter's decisions. His answer in support of his daughter drew criticism from antiabortion groups.

You can either say you refuse to speculate, or that at this point conjecture serves no useful purpose. You can try a humorous denial. Or like President Roosevelt, you too can suggest that you make it a point never to answer hypothetical questions.

PARAPHRASING QUESTIONS

Some of your responses to past questions could come back to haunt you at your current Q&A—in the form of the paraphrasing question. The problem here is that more often than not, the one asking it is in fact misinterpreting your words, thereby distorting your message. Sometimes, such a question is couched in the innocent phrase:

Did I understand you to say that . . .

Once it's apparent to you that you are confronted with a paraphrasing question, there's an easy way to deal with it. Simply take the onus on yourself and suggest, "No, that's not what I meant to say and let me apologize for not making myself clear. What I intended to suggest was . . ." Then go on to put your comments back on track. By using this approach you avoid offending the questioner who misunderstood your remarks. You also avoid blaming the media for misquoting you, a charge that often sounds hollow and self-serving. By accepting the blame yourself for miscommunicating, you earn the audience's goodwill in allowing you to set the record straight.

This exchange with a reporter by President Kennedy, on a fairly innocuous paraphrasing question, shows how Kennedy deflected it and gently reinforced his position. Note how he used the phrase "I think" to soften his response:

Reporter:
You once told us you had an opinion as to whether Mr. Nixon should enter the race for the California governorship, but you never told us what that was. Could you tell us?

John F. Kennedy:
I think I said at the time that I'd be glad to confide it to *him*, but he has just not as yet spoken to me about it (laughter). I'll have to go back to California and talk to him about that.

DART THROWERS

"Dart thrower" questions are those with negative implications built into them. These are usually blatantly critical of you or your organization. Here's a typical dart thrower question:

You know I've asked any number of irresponsible executives from your organization what you're going to do about your environmental problems. Now I'm asking you.

The tendency is to just answer the question. But by ignoring the negative dart thrust at you in the form of your executives being characterized as irresponsible (or insensitive or greedy or any other barb the questioner chooses to use) and by not challenging it, you tacitly accept this hostile label pinned on you.
The correct response?

Before I answer your question, I must take exception to your characterization of our executives. Far from being irresponsible, we've reacted swiftly and positively to all the environmental issues our organization has to deal with. Let me cite three or four specific examples for you.

Documenting the corrective action you've taken, using specific examples, validates your challenge to the questioner's choice of words while at the same time it answers the question.
As previously discussed, avoid generic, broad-stroke phrases such as "Your concern is our concern," or "We're also concerned about these issues." Without specifics to back them up, they remain empty, nonsupportable statements.
Frequently, someone—perhaps even a journalist—may ask you a question based on "misinformation." Again, if you simply answer the misinformer without first challenging the errone-

ous premise, you are in effect corroborating the erroneous information.

Again, politeness, restraint, and patience are called for. When confronted by a misinformer, you might simply say:

> With all due respect, our information runs counter to the premise suggested by your question. Let me tell you what our research shows.

A bit sharper but humorous approach was used by President Kennedy to deflect a rumor that he had cut a secret deal with the Soviets during a meeting in Moscow:

Reporter:
> The ranking house Republican expert on atomic energy says that in spite of all administration denials, he's sure there was a side agreement in Moscow. Is there some way you can present any proof positive?

John F. Kennedy:
> No, I cannot. There is nothing I can say other than to say that it isn't so. There's nothing the secretary of state can say other than that it isn't so. There's nothing Governor Harriman can say other than it isn't so. There's nothing that the prime minister of England who participated in the negotiations can say other than to say that it isn't so. . . . No, we cannot prove it.

In addition to using sarcasm to good effect to meet the charges of his detractors, Kennedy also was able to defend himself against his aggressors without getting into a detailed debate.

Reporter:
> A number of Republicans have questioned the qualifications of Franklin D. Roosevelt, Jr. to be the undersecretary of commerce. Would you like to answer them?

John F. Kennedy:
> Yes. They also questioned the qualifications of his father to be president (laughter). Mr. Roosevelt, I'm hopeful, will be confirmed. I wouldn't have sent him up there unless I felt he would be a good undersecretary. I hope the Senate confirms him.

Kennedy doesn't launch into a detailed examination of Roosevelt's qualifications for the job. That is not what is important here. He is not going to argue the case in front of the media. Instead, he does two things. One is to take a little wind out of the sails of his opponents by stating that "they also questioned the qualifications of his father to be president." The other is to affirm his personal support for his nominee.

RELATE QUESTIONS

The relate question is fairly common. Here, the individual merely frames a question drawn from events elsewhere in the news.

Aside from answering the question, the best way to prepare for the "relater" is to scan the most current news and anticipate any question that could be tied to those happenings and your topic. As mentioned in Part I, part of your rehearsal should be devoted to preparing a list of questions you're likely to be asked at the end of your talk, and making certain you have fully documented answers to those questions.

Frequently, people will ask you to comment on your critic's position. This can be a trap. If you fall into it, you can spend a lot of time restating those positions, in effect giving credence to the platforms of those who oppose you.

Don't! When confronted with a question asking you to react to the opinions of those who differ with you, simply respond by saying, "I'll let our opponents speak for themselves. Here is the way we see it." Then go on to espouse your own perspective. You could even preface that sentence with, "Someone once suggested if you don't have critics you're probably not doing your job. I'll let those who differ with us speak for themselves. Here's our perspective."

The objective is not to spend any time promoting the ideas of those who take issue with you. Rather, use those moments to reinforce your own ideas.

Consider President Kennedy's response to a reporter's baiting question during a press conference:

Reporter:
> General Eisenhower described the Republican party as the party of business. Now do you consider this fair or accurate as to the Republican party or to the business community?

John F. Kennedy:
> As I've said, I dislike disagreeing with President Eisenhower, so I won't in this case.

Kennedy retained control of the floor and drew the line at attacking the former president. He avoided having to defend himself or attack Eisenhower. This is a very tidy way of deflecting such a question.

Occasionally, someone from the audience might inquire about your personal feelings on a specific matter. The trap to avoid here is not to have a wedge divide your private and professional viewpoints.

Ideally, you should be able to have both perspectives mesh so you can then suggest on a personal level as well as a professional level, "I fully support what my organization is doing." That's utopia. But if you have difficulty reconciling your own feelings with those of the people you work for, simply say "I speak to you today solely as a representative of my organization and that's the perspective I will stick to."

WORST-CASE QUESTIONS

Worst-case questions invite you to walk the audience through the worst-case scenario. They ask you to recite chapter and verse on all that could go wrong. Worst-case questions are hypothetical in nature. But in order to reassure participants that you are aware of the potential dangers, you have to respond.

Here's an example of such a question:

> What else could go wrong here?

The best way to diffuse the potential negative impact of these questions is to answer them openly, honestly, completely, forthrightly, and candidly. But at the end, put it all in perspective by adding:

> That having been said, let me assure you that the likelihood of any of those eventualities ever materializing is the same as you and I getting hit by a meteor when we leave this gathering. It could happen. But I didn't lose any sleep last night worrying about it.

MACHINE-GUNNER QUESTIONS

"Machine-gunner" questions are multipart questions fired at you in such a rapid salvo that they can overwhelm you. These are three or four questions packed into one.

The strategy here is to simply pick one question out of the three or four that you're most comfortable with; the one question that most easily enables you to access your main point and reiterate it. Doing that allows you to emphasize the importance of your key message by responding with it first. Once you've satisfied your priority, you now have the choice of responding to the remaining unanswered questions, or you can simply throw them back to the machine gunner and say, "Now there were several other parts to your question—what were they?" Or you can simply continue to go forward and in any sequence you prefer to answer the balance of the remaining questions.

The key thing to note here is that you are in control. You call on whoever you wish and you answer the questions you're most comfortable handling. You also determine when the question-and-answer period is over.

Chapter Checklist

Anticipate Questions

How will you respond to each of the following types of questions?

- Close-ended   Answer as if it were open-ended.
- Hypothetical   Avoid unless in your interest.
- Paraphrasing   Clarify your past remarks.
- Dart thrower   Take exception to the comment, correct inaccuracies.
- Relate   Scan current news before speech.
- Worst-case   Be open, candid, positive.
- Machine gun   Take them one at a time.

Death by Oratory

The questioner asks a very detailed question about corporate problems. The speaker either responds in tremendous detail or deflects the question. Either way, the speaker loses the initiative. If, instead, the speaker responds with humor or a general explanation, the speaker retains control of the floor, provides some information, and so successfully responds.

- Don't let your questioner bait you into answering a question that makes you uncomfortable or forces you to reveal information that you prefer not to reveal.

- Don't deliberately avoid answering questions or appear to be arrogant. This can be more damaging than any answer you might give.

- Don't miss the opportunity to reinforce your key themes during the Q&A.

Chapter Eighteen

Make Friends

I t's important in the Q&A to never lose your composure. This format gives you one last opportunity to influence your audience, one last opportunity to make lots of friends. You can easily blow it by blowing your cool. Don't! Even when confronted with skepticism or outright hostility, don't get angry. Maintain your composure, your professional demeanor.

As a speechgiver, you are a teacher. You'll recall that the best teachers you had were probably the ones who were patient with their students' lack of understanding. They were the ones who kept coming up with alternative ways to explain their material until eventually even the most confused student was able to comprehend it. And they did it with kindness, with restraint, and yes, even love.

That must be your demeanor at all times during presentations. Care enough about even the most cantankerous questioners so as to increase the odds of their coming around to accepting your ideas. Because you have the microphone, you have much more power than anyone in the audience. That means your questioner can often be perceived as the underdog. This can create a situation in which the entire audience turns against you—even if they agree with your position.

In sum, don't get angry. Make friends.

REPEATING THE QUESTION

It's a good idea—both as a tactic and as a courtesy—to repeat each question. As a tactic, it gives you time to frame your answer while you're repeating the question. It even allows you to just slightly rephrase the question without altering its meaning so you can reemphasize your main message.

Repeating the question is also a courtesy to those people in the audience who may be sitting far away from the individual who asked it and may not have heard the issues raised. If the questioner is a machine gunner who fires off several questions in succession, repeating the questions also makes it clear which question you are answering.

USING NAMES

The post-presentation question-and-answer period is an ideal time to make friends and gain sympathizers to your cause.

Using first names is one way to do just that. Suggest at the outset that the questioners you call on should give their names and affiliations. The more you know about each person, and the more information you have about that individual's organization, the easier it will be to frame an acceptable answer.

Using the first name sets an informal and pleasant tone. It suggests friendship. It suggests kinship.

This technique works especially well when someone from the audience challenges you. Responding with that person's first name subtly blunts the thrust of that challenge. However, if you think it might be inappropriate to use a first name, use no name at all.

Avoid using surnames, even if yours is used by the questioner. Remember, you're not only answering the person making the inquiry. You're also talking to everyone else in that room. Using surnames sets up walls of formality—perhaps even impenetrable barriers—that may inhibit such contact.

USE YOUR SENSE OF HUMOR

Don't overlook the use of humor. Act like you are enjoying yourself. Better yet, try to enjoy yourself. So many speakers approach the Q&A as if it's an interrogation or a trial. It's not—at least, it shouldn't be. But if you start responding like a defendant, your audience may sound more and more like a district attorney.

So many pernicious questions can be deflected with humor. Unless the audience is after your head, humor will work well in the Q&A. Listen to this exchange by President John F. Kennedy during a press conference in the 1960s:

Reporter:
Mr. President, your brother Ted recently on television said that after seeing the cares of office on you, he wasn't sure if he'd ever be interested in being president. I wonder if you could tell us whether if you had it to do over again, whether you would work for the presidency and if you would recommend the job to others?
John F. Kennedy:
The first answer is yes, and the second is no. I don't recommend it to others—at least not for a while.

The room burst into laughter. Instead of giving a deep, soul-searching answer, Kennedy demonstrated his sense of humor at the same time that he retained control over the situation. A sense of humor allows you to remain on the offensive. It also keeps the atmosphere relaxed and shows that you can exhibit grace under pressure. Remember, it is not what you say as much as how you say it that will leave a lasting impression on your audience.

At the same time, never turn your humor against your questioners or against other people. This will make you look malicious. Instead, look for the humor in the question itself.

Also, don't use humor on a serious question if it will appear that you are brushing off the questioner. You might reply with humor initially and then follow with a straightforward statement. But if you do not feel comfortable answering a question, humor can be a way to put it off, without becoming defensive. It can be more graceful to say "My lawyers won't allow me to talk about that" or "I plead the fifth on that one," rather than a stonefaced: "I can't comment on that at this time."

If you don't have the stamina or wit to carry off humor, at least try to smile. A smile will show you are relaxed and also make your audience more relaxed. It shows you are comfortable.

Practice smiling. It doesn't take any great skill and will be sure to make an impression on the audience.

Ultimately, you are there to entertain and inform, not to protect yourself. Humor in the question-and-answer session shows that you are willing to let down your guard a little. It implies that you are comfortable with the questions. Just like at a political debate, people listen not so much to obtain information as to see the speaker in action. Because the biggest question an audience has is whether you can stand up under pressure, whether your ideas can withstand the scrutiny of cross-examination.

That question, you can answer with a smile.

DEBATES

Sometimes, irrespective of how kind, patient, and honest you are during the Q&A process, through no fault of your own you may find yourself in a confrontation. This can either be a friendly exchange of differing positions or it can disintegrate into a hostile debate. The more you maintain your composure, the more likely it is that the rest of the audience will align themselves with you.

I remember once after a presentation I made in Chicago, I found myself the object of the wrath of one particular audience member. It was clear to me that "Don" was taking many of the frustrations accumulated from other parts of his life out on me.

My answers mattered little. Irrespective of what I said, Don had his little speeches to make and clearly nothing I would say or do was going to stop him.

It wasn't easy. But I stayed calm. At one point, I'd surmised Don was not fully in control of his reasoning, and as I listened to him lash out at me for the second or third time, I made up my mind not to call on him again. Then, unexpectedly, from the audience I heard:

Oh, sit down, Don!
Shut up, Don!
Give it up, Don!

Clearly, the audience took my side, and because I remained calm and polite, I maintained their respect and support, which usually happens when you are a guest—as most speakers are—in someone else's house.

So much for irrational outbursts. Often, you will find a vociferous person with a legitimate challenge to your viewpoints.

If so, first seek out areas of agreement, showing that you and your opponent are not really that far apart. Something like:

> Well, we don't really disagree on what needs to be done, just on how to do it. So we're not that far apart after all.

This strategy tends to blunt the thrust of your critic's position.

Another strategy is to question the sources of your challenger's information. Using this technique puts your opponents on the defensive and forces them to respond to you.

> I question your premise, Helen. What's the source of your information?

Now Helen has to answer your question. She's on the defensive and will remain there as long as you keep asking her questions. Eventually, when she's been discredited, you can stop asking her questions and summarize the entire discussion with a sample statement in support of your position.

President John F. Kennedy used such an approach when he was accused of managing the news in the following exchange with a reporter:

Reporter:
> Mr. President, the practice of managed news is attributed to your administration. Mr. Salinger says, he's never had it defined. Would you give us your definition and tell us why you find it necessary to practice it?

John F. Kennedy:
> You are charging us with something, Miss Gray, and then you are asking me to define what it is you are charging me with. Let me just say that we have had very limited success in managing the news if that's what we've been trying to do. Perhaps you'd tell us what it is you object to in our treatment of the news.

Reporter:
Well, I don't believe in managed news at all. I think we ought to get everything we want.

John F. Kennedy:
I think that too, Miss Gray. I'm for that.

Kennedy continued to retain control of the conversation. He appeared so helpful and solicitous, but at the same time he deflated the question by stating that they "have had very limited success." He threw the question back to the questioner. And the whole thrust fizzled. If he had been defensive, the exchange might have ended differently.

Remember that when you're at the lectern, you are in control. It is not a democracy. You can call on anyone at any time. You can finish your answer and then quickly move on to the next question, leaving no time for rebuttal. You decide when to end the proceedings. But it should be a benevolent dictatorship. If you abuse your power, the audience will take its only recourse—to stop listening.

Sometime you may find yourself the target of a heckler. Or someone may ask you a sensitive question:

As a result of the chemicals your company makes, my brother who used to work for you handling those chemicals is dying. What are you going to do about it?

A good choice here is to respond by suggesting perhaps this isn't the best forum for discussing this issue, or for responding to personal problems. Explain that you'll be happy to personally look into the matter. Suggest that you and the heckler or the individual with a sensitive personal problem get together one on one after the group breaks up. That way, you appear to be responsive without prolonging your being on the defensive publicly as the target of someone who is angry or upset.

Finally, a word on interruptions. You may be in the middle of a good solid point, reinforcing the messages made in your speech. At the same time, you may find yourself continually being interrupted by one or more members of the audience.

If the interrupter is the person you called on to ask a question, simply respond by saying:

Carl, let me finish answering your previous question before we move on. You had asked me . . .

Should Carl persist, I would repeat that same phrase exactly the way you had articulated it the first time. Carl should eventually back down and cease interrupting. If not, you can finally remind him that as the invited speaker, you're also an invited guest and as such would be grateful for the courtesy and the opportunity to finish—without interruption.

Should the interruptions come from a variety of different members of the audience, then you have to remind them that in order to effect a coherent exchange of ideas, it's best they wait their turn, and that you as chairperson will do your best to make certain everyone is heard from before the proceedings end.

CHOOSING THE RIGHT WORDS

In addition to being lured into debates, there are other common pitfalls among Q&A presenters that you can easily avoid. A major source of problems is in the choice of words. Often, spontaneous responses can be repetitious, ineffective, and even inflammatory. You don't have the time to carefully craft responses as you do when preparing a speech. You can rehearse potential answers to questions, but you also have to be more vigilant about the exact words you use. By paying careful attention to your use of words and the impact of different word choices, you can keep your words fresh and exciting without raising alarms.

Repetitive Phrases

Repeating one phrase can be distracting and irritating. Perhaps my ear is too sensitive, but on a national business show segment lasting roughly eight minutes, I heard an economic forecaster start no less than 13 sentences with the word *well*. The echo was so bad, he might have been speaking from the bottom of a well. Talk about annoying.

In addition to *well*, some other overworked phrases include *you know, okay,* and *now.*

The best way to find out if you're overworking phrases is to tape a few of your presentations and play them back with the express view of weeding out those phrases and words that add nothing but tedium to your remarks. And while you are looking for those repeated words, also keep an eye out for empty promises, discredited phrases, and inflammatory words.

Empty Promises

These phrases suggest you're doing something constructive by addressing a problem but offer little by way of specifics—in other words, ways to solve the problem. "We're concerned about . . ." is perhaps the classic empty promise phrase, unless it's followed up with specific solutions:

> We're concerned about the environment—so much so that we've developed new ways to dispose of chemical wastes. I'd like to tell you about them.

Unless you have such documentation, avoid using that phrase.

Discredited Phrases

"No comment" is perhaps the classic discredited phrase. By not commenting, you become guilty by default in the audience's mind. If you can't comment, you must explain why and then go on to talk about something you can discuss:

> I can't comment on that because, as you may know, we're in litigation and we're only going to try this case in a court of law. But what I can say is . . .

Inflammatory Phrases

Inflammatory words and phrases should especially be avoided when you or your organization are in trouble. They are stark words and could make a tragedy seem worse. For example, as opposed to saying "six people were killed" or "six people died," say "there were six fatalities."

Examples of other inflammatory words to avoid are:

- Devastated (versus destroyed).
- Annihilated (versus perished).
- Disaster (versus trouble).
- Crushed (as opposed to buried beneath).

Although these are phrases you would probably instinctively avoid in your formal remarks, you need to be vigilant to ensure that they do not creep into your answers to questions.

There is certainly a role for these words in the vernacular. In a presentation, however, they should be used sparingly and only to describe a worst-case scenario. On the other hand, don't use weasel words, as noted in Chapter 6. If euphemisms are too far from reality, they can undermine the credibility of the speaker. So handle these phrases with care.

Chapter Checklist

Make Friends

- Think of yourself as a teacher in answering questions from the audience.
- Repeat the question.
- Use first names.
- Avoid debates.
- Choose words carefully to avoid repetition, empty promises, discredited phrases, and inflammatory phrases.

Death by Oratory

The speaker is locked in conflict with a heckler in the audience. The speaker's voice is rising as he attempts to shout down his accuser. But the accuser just attacks more vehemently. It is too late. The speaker brings the Q&A to an abrupt conclusion and storms off the stage, flustered and angry.

- Don't get drawn into a debate.
- Don't take anything that is said personally, even if it is a personal attack.
- Don't lose your temper or abuse your power on the podium.
- Don't lose control. You have the floor. You decide how to answer questions and which questions to take.

Conclusion

Take a bow. You've made it through the preparation, performance, and Q&A. And you haven't died.

The more you practice the techniques outlined in this book, the more they will become second nature. You will find yourself automatically looking for a good grabber to launch your speech. You won't be able to plan a speech without thinking about road maps. You'll be constantly listening for phrases with ear appeal, or ways to use numbers and humor. You'll be paying attention to your own life, looking for interesting stories. When you go to write your next speech, you may find you have more than enough material accumulated through this process.

Most of all, you can begin listening to other speeches, to see how speakers have applied these and other principles. You can also see where they have failed to follow these approaches, and how they have suffered for it.

As we stressed at the closing of Part I, there is no way to create an instant speech that is successful. It takes hard work and perseverance. But it is worth it.

Your ability to speak clearly, concisely, and convincingly in public can have a powerful, positive impact on your life and your career.

Finally, a word about *fun*. On a national television show, performer Harry Connick, Jr. talked about the emotional surge he gets from performing. He discussed the energy and the excitement, along with the thrill of being in control while making people feel good.

Use and perfect the techniques suggested here, and you, too, should feel the joy of performing, the rewards of persuading.

You're on!

(Applause. Fade to black.)

Endnotes

1. A. Nevins, *The Burden and the Glory* (New York: Harper & Row, 1964), pp. 98–99.
2. C. M. Howard, "Perestroika from Pleasantville: Lessons Learned Launching *Reader's Digest* in the Soviet Union and Hungary," The Conference Board, Corporate Image Conference, January 28–29, 1992.
3. K. E. Weick, "Substitutes for Strategy," in *The Competitive Challenge: Strategies for Industrial Innovation and Renewal*, ed. David J. Teece (New York: Ballinger Books, 1987), p. 222.
4. Nevins, *The Burden and the Glory*, p. 100.
5. A. Stevenson, "The City—A Cause for Statesmanship," in *The Speaker's Resource Book*, ed. Carroll C. Arnold, Douglas Ehninger, and John C. Gerber (Glenview, Ill.: Scott, Foresman, 1961), p. 224.
6. M. L. King, Jr., "I Have a Dream," in *The Speaker's Resource Book*, pp. 152–56.
7. D. MacArthur, "Address to Congress," in *The Speaker's Resource Book*, p. 284.
8. G. V. Grune, "The Power of a Great Magazine," speech to *Reader's Digest* Global Editorial Conference, Lake George, NY. June 2, 1991.
9. Robert J. Baer, remarks to United Exchange, February 27, 1990.
10. C. D. Keen, "May You Live in Interesting Times," in *Executive Speeches*, April 1992.
11. M. Pred, speech to Nebraska Food Industry Association, November 4, 1992.
12. R. Reilly, personal correspondence to the author, December 12, 1992.
13. V. Gregorian, Preface to *The New York Public Library Desk Reference* (New York: Songstone Press, 1989), p. xi.

14. G. V. Grune, "Going Global in the New World," speech to the Economic Club of Detroit. March 9, 1992.

15. J. T. Flexner, *Washington: The Indispensable Man* (Boston: Little, Brown, 1974).

16. "Thoughts on the Business Life," *Forbes*, October 19, 1992, p. 296.

Index

More Business Books From Carol Publishing Group